INTRODUCING
FEMINIST IMAGES OF GOD

INTRODUCING

FEMINIST IMAGES OF GOD

Mary Grey

 INTRODUCTIONS IN **FEMINIST** THEOLOGY

EDITORIAL COMMITTEE

Mary Grey • Lisa Isherwood

Catherine Norris • Janet Wootton

The Pilgrim Press

Cleveland, Ohio

Published in the USA and Canada (only) by

The Pilgrim Press, Cleveland, Ohio 44115

© 2001 by Sheffield Academic Press

Originally published by Sheffield Academic Press, Ltd., Sheffield, England

The Pilgrim Press edition published 2001. All rights reserved.

Printed in Great Britain on acid-free paper

06 05 04 03 02 01   5 4 3 2 1

ISBN 0-8298-1418-3

Table of Contents

Introduction

It is a daunting task to begin a book about God. It seems arrogant—maybe divine disapproval will carry me off in the course of it! Should I wait, like Elijah in the cave (1 Kgs 19) for a revelation as to how to write? No angel sits at my elbow with chapter headings—although I believe the air is resonant with angelic insights... I hesitate for another reason: relationship with God is highly personal, yet I am asked to write about a movement which every day grows more complex.

So I make certain decisions. As I am a committed Christian, I write principally about the Christian feminist new imaging of God, a movement I have been actively engaged in for the last thirteen years. The two exceptions are that I discuss the Goddess movement because of its links with Christian feminism (and, briefly, Jewish feminism's naming of God, because of Christianity's roots in Judaism) and because of the parallels in the process of naming.[1] Although I make every effort to be true to the wider process, I know that in the selection I make, in the criteria I choose, and the examples I give, I reveal my own views. The reader will judge if this is intrusive. Only in the epilogue do I write freely from my own convictions—yet even there I had to resist the urge to develop my own views. But that would have been another kind of book.

To my surprise, this book has taken much longer than anticipated—and I am thankful that my co-editors, Lisa, Janet and Catherine, as well as Sheffield Academic Press have been generous in their lack of complaint! I owe so much to the patience and careful attention of my desk editor, Sarah Norman. Trying to take a distance from a movement in which I am so engaged was not easy, but I am grateful for the challenge to think critically about what is happening.

I owe much to so many people for many of the insights here. I would like to thank my friends and colleagues in many women's groups, from BISFT (British and Irish School of Feminist Theology), the Synod

---

1. I am a member of ICCJ (International Committee of Christians and Jews, and for ten years have participated in a dialogue with Jewish women).

groups—in Europe and Britain, not forgetting the Austrian group—and Michaela's energy!—the European Academy at Boldern, Switzerland with its inspiring leaders, Reinhild Traitler and Elisabeth Raiser, to the women from Satya Shodak in Bombay, India—especially Crescy John, to Carol Boulter of *Women Church*, Berkshire (which we founded together), and to the Liturgy Group meeting in my own home, especially Gillian whose enthusiasm keeps me going. Participating in these worshipping groups and receiving the gifts of such creative people has, I hope, given this book its authenticity as rooted in the lives of real people. I want to thank Nicholas especially, for enduring my frequent absences at our meetings, as well as my absorption in the writing process, as I tried this year to finish two books—and for believing that my writing mattered.

I would like to dedicate this book to Professor Catherina Halkes, the first Professor of Feminism and Christianity in Nijmegen, the Netherlands. Because you always believed that it was possible to be a feminist and a worshipping believer in God, you remain an inspiration, Tine, and I am blessed in being still in relation, *verbonden,*[2] with you.

---

2. 'Verbonden' means *connected with, in relation with*.

Chapter One

Struggling to Move 'Beyond God the Father'

She say, my first step from the old white man was trees. Then air. Then birds. Then other people. But one day when I was sitting quiet, like a motherless child, which I was, it come to me: that feeling of being part of everything, not separate at all. I knew that if I cut a tree, my arm would bleed (Walker 1983: 167).

Where to begin? is always the burning question. So much of both Western feminist thinking as well as that of women of colour and women in the struggle for justice on a worldwide basis was sparked off by the critique of *Beyond God the Father* (Daly 1973)—even if it was to disagree with its author!—which seemed to touch a very deep chord. It was a chord which energized women (and increasingly, men) to articulate resistance to the powerful grip that patriarchy held on culture's dominant symbols and images.

First of all, perhaps the strongest conviction (at least of the Euro-American feminists who began the initial analysis of the problem during the last 30 years), was that the traditional symbolism of *God the Father* (together with all associated imagery, as well as the fact of the male identity of Jesus), functioned to exclude women and to exclude female imagery from being able to symbolize the divine (Ruether 1983). It reinforced the supposition (both hidden and explicit in key texts) that maleness is normative for humanity: 'he is the subject, she is the other', as the famous saying went (de Beauvoir 1973: 16). Femaleness was defined relative to, in opposition to, or complementary to maleness. None of these options inspired a free-standing female symbol system, a female cultural imaginary, which could reflect the range of possibilities and complexity of being a woman in all the diversity of race, culture, class, sexual preference, social possibilities, health and so on. Throughout history this has meant that justification for the leadership, authority and participation of women in society has had almost no theoretical underpinning. In Christian theological terms, it meant not only that women had no role models for the full becoming of women, calling into question the whole significance of the Mystery of the Incarnation for women,[1] but also that the exclusively male images for God (father, judge, lord, king, warrior) were embodied and legitimized by the power structures of patriarchal or *kyriarchal*[2] society. Even though the developments of feminist theology in the last 30 years have moved on from universalist assumptions of global sisterhood to focus far more on differences between women—of culture, experience, context and the analysis of oppressive situations—yet the controlling influence of patriarchal–kyriarchal power on women's lives, as well as on the lives of many indigenous peoples, in myriads of destructive forms, is living testimony that exclusively male imagery for the divine is still a crucial issue.

The cultural effects of this imagery may well often be hidden, but in a *macho* society, where violence prevails on a public level, it can be glaringly evident. For example, in countries under oppressive military dictatorships, masculinity is linked with military and sexual violence: the young soldier is trained in a context which separates him from warm, intimate relationships with his family, and women in particular. Sexuality then becomes inextricably linked with violence (Thistlethwaite 1996). Yet, far from being restricted to Third World contexts, husbands abusing wives and children, being violent or abandoning their families is a global phenomenon and much wider than the military context alone. In fact, the existence of violent and abusive behaviour of fathers towards their children has made some question of whether we do now, after all, desperately still need a redeemed *father* image for God, since the human analogue seems to be failing so badly. In a sensitive article, the theologian Janet Martin Soskice asked if a feminist can in fact call God 'Father' (Soskice 1992). Perhaps, in the end, what Jesus was doing by his own name for God, a term of endearment, 'Abba', was indeed to rid 'Father' of patriarchal, controlling, distant and violent overtones. As we begin our examination of feminist names for God, it is important to

1.   This would eventually be thematized in a powerful way by Luce Irigaray (1985). It is also the spur to the project of Grace Jantzen in developing a fully-fledged feminist philosophy of religion (Jantzen 1998).

2.   The word *kyriarchy* was coined by Elisabeth Schüssler Fiorenza, and means the 'rule of the Lord', thus comprehending in one word the oppression of gender, race and class.

remember that Jesus himself in this way entered the process of 'new naming'. With this possibility of reclaiming a 'good' father image, it is also timely to consider whether in fact the 'Father' God considered to be so excluding and harmful to the becoming of women is *not* actually the authentic God of Judaism or Christianity. Is 'He' a distortion, a projection or caricature needed by societies for whom it was convenient to adhere to male dominance and control of power? A concept of male dominance that required the subordination, limited participation and damaging (even demonizing) stereotyping of women?

However much progress as regards the position of women there is in certain countries (*some* but by no means *all*), in other parts of the world the position of women is still far from having achieved equal status and in some cases more than a very basic level of respect. In India, the low worth of the girl-child by comparison with the boy (because of the cost she brings in needing a dowry for marriage) has meant the steady rise of girl infanticide, or abortion. The AIDS pandemic—in India as well as Africa—has increased the number of young girls sold into prostitution, or the flesh-trade, as it is now called. Even the fact of divine imagery in the shape of Hindu goddesses does not necessarily have a positive effect on the lives of these women and girls: mostly the goddess is revered as a part of a patriarchal religious system, so that she functions to control women and keep them subordinate.[3]

In Euro-American societies, where liberal ideals of equality are theoretically promoted and put into practice, actively campaigning for the position of women across a variety of work situations, public institutions and faith communities, now seems to have lost 'bite', or all sense of urgency. Women are generally considered to be enjoying a high level of freedom and participation in institutions (education, medical, legal profession and so on) (and sometimes do)—never mind that it is poor women of colour who are usually cleaning the office blocks late at night or early morning, and receiving very low levels of pay.

---

3. The situation is actually far more complex: there are ways in which women can and do reverence the goddess figures, seeking courage and strength to endure. For example, Phoolan Devi, the Bandit Queen—who endured child marriage with an abusive man, gang rape, the murder of her bandit king lover—prayed to Durga, the Mother Goddess, before a decisive event (Sen 1991). Indian feminist re-envisioning of the myths is now contributing to more empowering versions. See Baltazar 1996.

But, by contrast, in the churches—with some exceptions—the same struggles for recognition and participation carry on. Even in those churches who do ordain women,[4] and admit them to decision-making structures, the legacy of thousands of years of exclusive male symbols, and exclusive use of power does not disappear overnight. For example, in conservative circles—where appeals to 'tradition' have always been the norm—the revered status of the Father symbol has not only been unquestioned, but has strengthened its position, sometimes even in protest against feminist theological attempts at new imagery. (This has occurred on many occasions, even when a female, scripturally-authorized image has been introduced in the most sensitive manner.) Usually, this reinforcing of traditional images goes hand in hand with the reaffirming of traditional roles of women in both church and society, with an emphasis on the importance of the family and motherhood.

Who are the Voices Calling for Change?

One arena where the current calling for change is growing to a mighty surge is in the area of liturgy.[5] Imagine the scene here in Europe. You are a devoted female Christian. Yet—despite a very few alterations to liturgical prayer, or unless you happen to be in a very enlightened liturgical setting (and they do exist! I do not want to underestimate the efforts of liturgists for change)—week after week you listen to Scripture calling you to the freedom of the 'sons of God'; you hear that Christ died for all men; you sing a vast selection of hymns in which you are not addressed, and in which male images are piled on top of each other; what is more, you listen to sermons which do not touch your experience. If you are black, you feel doubly non-addressed by the trappings of a eurocentric Christianity, and might have been driven to join one of the black-led churches.

I have never yet heard a sermon in a Roman Catholic parish church which condemned male violence against women, or even touched the

---

4.   The Church of Scotland, for example, has ordained women for over 20 years, as has the United Reform Church. The vote for the ordination of women in the Church of England was passed on 11 November 1992, and in Wales in 1997. The Orthodox Churches remain in opposition. The Roman Catholic Church has declared that the ordination of women will never be a possibility.

5.   See, in this series, Wootton 2000.

theme of sexual abuse or which tackled white racism and prejudice—although this is now being addressed to some extent, for example, by the introduction of Racial Justice Sunday. It is also addressed by some non-conformist churches, by the black-led churches, and increasingly by the preaching of women where this is encouraged. However, the economic realities of people's lives often remain invisible—even though the entire preaching of Jesus was embedded in the very visible poverty of his community. All my life I have searched and struggled for vibrant forms of Christian community.[6] And I witness a constant stream of women (and men) leaving the Church here in Europe because of its failure to speak to their lives, its insistence on a rigid, inflexible adherence to expressions of faith, styles of worship, and its merciless attitudes to those whose life situation cannot conform to its edicts.

Yet, sometimes I see the contrary in a breakthrough of extraordinary grace. I see Christian communities entering a dynamic, liberating phase when inclusive images and liturgies are experienced. In England I think of the creative liturgies of the Association for Inclusive Language (AIL), and the liturgies of the Catholic Women's Network (CWN). Every first Wednesday of the month, the Catholic Women for Ordination (CWO) group hold a simple liturgy of symbolic action in the piazza outside Westminster Cathedral in London. The We are Church movement is committed to a vibrant church of life, constantly protesting against the abuse of human rights in the Church, power exercised in an autocratic, absolutist way, and the denial of ordination to women and married men.[7] We are Church is linked with Wir Sind Kirche (Austria), Somos Iglesia (Spain), Nous sommes Église (France) and the International Movement We are Church (IMWAC). In a European context, I think of the worship of the European Forum of Ecumenical Christian Women (EFECW), and on an international basis, those of the Decade of the Churches in Solidarity with Women (1988–1998) and the Synodical movement which has now sprung up at the end of this decade.[8] All of these are examples of groups challenging the hierarchical, clerical, male, absolutist and elitist model of the Church.

6.   See Grey (1997, 1997a).

7.   A wider interfaith context would be the Women's Seminars of the International Council for Christians and Jews (ICCJ).

8.   The first pan-European Synod took place in 1996; the first British WISE Women's Synod in 1999, at Liverpool Hope College. (WISE = Wales, Ireland, Scotland, England.)

And this is not to forget the wider network: the many communities who are meeting and experiencing an empowering presence of the sacred as they either re-envision Christian, Islamic and Jewish Scriptures from an inclusive, justice-oriented perspective, or widen the horizons to include other sacred texts. And these groups would include Justice and Peace groups who are open to a wider perspective, individuals like Jim Cotter, who speaks to the pain and anguish of many people, whose prayers offer support for the experiences of despair and abandonment in the is darkness of the night (Cotter 1983, 1999). The voices of lesbian and gay groups, and the ministry to AIDS people have now broken the silence in poignant and distinctive tones (Stuart 1992, 1995); and the many ecology groups, painfully aware that care for the environment is also a forgotten dimension, speak for the earth which has no voice. What unites these groups is a sense that traditional forms of imaging of God and style of worship fail to ignite the fire that turns the human spirit to deeper faith and action. Yet, at the same time, it is a deep faith in God and belief in the empowerment of community worship that fuel this search for authentic forms of worship. Rosemary Radford Ruether once, famously, referred to the Eucharistic famine from which we all suffer (Ruether 1985: 4-5). Need for nurture prompts the search for liberating community; but loyalty to the church means that women and men continue to put effort into traditional parishes while, where they can, finding their real inspirational community elsewhere.

But the second source for re-imaging, already alluded to, is the conviction of the link between images of the Deity and responsible ethical action. Even though the expression 'God's in Heaven—all's right with the world' is no longer believed in by anyone, and is seen as a misleading guarantor of the status quo, yet the feeble power of traditional images to work for the transformation of society is a powerful stimulant for change. As Carter Heyward writes, God is a God who 'drives to justice and makes it' (Heyward 1982: 162). But the distant male, all-powerful God, the Christ who is linked with the power-structures of Western society and the all-male Trinity so critiqued by Mary Daly (Daly 1973: 114-22) have actually been used as a deterrent for the justice-making processes! 'God on our side, blessing the bombers for Vietnam' is a horrific image from the 1960s. God is frequently invoked on the side or order, uniformity, and preserver of the status quo. Nor can preserving the earth, apparently, necessarily be considered part of God's plan.

According to American 'apocalyptic' thinking of the Reagan regime of the 1980s, we do not need to endure too much angst about our planet, as, like a spoilt child who loses 'his' toy, *Daddy will give us a new one!* (Keller 1990: 250). Ultimately, so the thinking goes, the promise of the new Jerusalem as humanity's final home, means that this earth is disposable. It plays no part in eternal dimensions.

But when Jesus preached his vision of the Kingdom of God, he used familiar images and symbols belonging to this earth—the mustard seed, the wheat and the cockle, the yeast—in such a way as to include groups of people on the edges of respectability, without status or power—the lepers, the women and children, and ethnic groups treated with suspicion (for example, Samaritans, the Syro-Phoenician woman, the Roman centurion). So it is not surprising to find that to break out of what has seemed an impasse in thinking about God, a surge of creativity—springing from the praxis of lived faith—blazes a trail.

Imagining a New Symbolic World

Breaking out of what seemed like a strait-jacket in thinking about God, poets, artists and musicians have led the way. No strict categories can or should be fixed on these attempts. Here I do not embark on a critique or a neat tidying into existing theological categories—but in successive chapters I will try to reflect theologically on new developments. Here I want to try to paint a picture of the range of images emerging from women's struggle for justice and a 'brave new world'.

First, a whole range of images and symbols tries to counteract the maleness of God with God imagined as female. I think of Meinrad Craighead's paintings of God-as-Mother giving birth to the world (Hurcombe 1987), of attempts to image an inclusive Trinity (God as creator, pain-bearer and lover), and of Janet Morley's beautiful re-writing of the psalms with God as mother and lover as the heart:

> I will praise God, my Beloved,
> for she is altogether lovely.
>
> Her presence satisfies my soul;
> she fills my senses to overflowing
> so that I cannot speak (Morley 1988: 50).

And also of Brian Wren's bringing together of many of these images:

Who is She,
  neither male nor female,
    maker of all things,
    only glimpsed or hinted,
  source of life and gender?
She is God,
  mother, sister, lover;
    in her love we wake,
    move and grow, are daunted,
  triumph and surrender.

Who is She,
  mothering her people,
    teaching them to walk,
    lifting weary toddlers,
  bending down to feed them?
She is Love,
  crying in a stable,
    teaching in a boat,
  friendly with the lepers,
  bound for crucifixion.

Who is She,
  sparkle in the rapids,
    coolness of the well,
    living power of Jesus
  flowing from the scriptures?
She is Life,
  water, wind and laughter,
    calm, yet never still,
  swiftly moving Spirit,
  singing in the changes.

Why is She,
  mother of all nature,
    longing for birth,
    gasping yet exulting
  to a new creation?
She is Hope,
  never tired of loving,
    filling all with worth,
    glad of our achieving,
  lifting all to freedom.
(Wren 1989: 141-42).[9]

The reclaiming of the image of the Mother God spans all the religions as well as inspiring ecological, earth-based spiritualities. (This will be the focus of Chapter 2.) What unites these many attempts is the need to discover an embodied God, a God who does not despise material, sexual and bodily realities. Hence Shug's assertion in *The Colour Purple* (Walker 1983: 167):

God love all those things—God made them.

This is a God who heals the abused flesh of women. A God who hears the cries of poor women who cannot feed their children, who is present for the violated woman who cannot flee from violence because there is nowhere to go.

One of the ways this is expressed is in a well-known inspirational form—'I found God within myself, and I loved her, I loved her fiercely' (Shange 1976: 63), bringing together the need to discover God who is not an abstraction but deep within (a new and more dynamic form of immanence than is usually implied), as part of the recovery of self-

9.   Brian Wren ©1986 Stainer & Bell Ltd, London, England. Reproduced from 'Piece Together Praise'.

esteem, the journey to healed sexuality and wholeness. It is no coincidence that this was the utterance of a black woman: much of the spirituality arising from womanist theology expresses the double pain of being despised as woman together with being despised as black woman. Nor should 'I found God within myself' be understood in an individualist way. As Shug says:

> God is inside of you and inside everybody else. You come into the world with God. But only them that search for it inside find it (Walker 1983: 177).

Many of the images of God we shall discuss from Latin America, Asia and Africa share the yearning, the burning anger, and the unquenchable hopes that God is a God of justice, who will liberate communities of poor women—with their children, sons, menfolk and the land so necessary to survival—in the concreteness of the particular struggle. A strong focus on an immanent God surfaces, for example, in Argentina—as Jesus, the *companēro*, the struggling brother in history, a focus we shall see also in womanist spirituality. Jesus as God in history has also been imaged as a woman since the earliest Christian times: not only has this occurred through the Christa image of Edwina Sandys, or the Toronto Christa[10] but also through the Indian artist, Lucy de Souza's picture of Christ/Christa the Tree of Life, and Christ the Generation Tree of the Shona people of Zimbabwe. Here Jesus is a man—we know it from his beard—yet his body is that of a woman, and he carries a baby on his back, like an African mother working in the fields. Emerging from this conviction that God is struggling with poor women for justice in the historical struggle is a spirituality of resistance (to the status quo, the structures of colonialism and any compromise with them), of hope and of life. It is this rootedness in a God of life, which inspires praying and acting out of many images of the divine, some of which spring from pre-Christian sources.

Yet another series of images springs from the consciousness that all language about God is analogical and metaphorical. Sallie McFague has made this the lynch pin of her theology, in her groundbreaking explo-

---

10. This was donated by an artist to the Memorial Chapel of Bloor St United Church, Toronto: 'This Christa caused heated discussion within Victoria University, so much so that it was decided to place the suffering woman in the backyard of Emmanuel College, Toronto…however, after the University of Montreal massacre in 1989, when eleven women were gunned down, an annual memorial for the victims has been held in her presence. So the statue is now linked directly to that event and has come to symbolise it on campus' (see Grey 1997b: 192).

rations of new metaphors (McFague 1982, 1987, 1993, 1997). In more than ten years of development she moves from exploring God as mother, friend and lover, to seeing the world *as* 'The Body of God'—although, of course, this had been explored earlier by Grace Jantzen (Jantzen 1984). When we call God 'Father'—according to 'official' theology—we do not mean it literally. Usually people will go along thus far with us; but when it is suggested that we pray to God the Mother, there is a swift withdrawal: 'Oh no, we cannot pray to God the Mother—of course God is our Father!'

Thus, some attempts to re-image God try to rise beyond the male/female split. So, in a way similar to Paul Tillich's naming God as *ultimate concern, ground of all being* (but mindful of Mary Daly's dismissal of this as ignoring the being of women and their struggle to be accepted as full human subjects [Daly 1973: 72, 127, 128]), Rosemary Ruether thinks of God as God/ess, as the cosmic matrix of all being, to which we return after death:

> That great matrix that supports the great energy-matter of our individu-ated being, is itself the ground of all personhood as well. That great col-lective personhood is the Holy Being in which our achievements and failures are gathered up, assimilated into the fabric of being and carried into new possibilities (Ruether 1983: 258).

Carter Heyward also constructs an inclusive view of God, while envi-sioning God as the heart of the struggle for justice, as the 'power of right relation' (Heyward 1982), the power of erotic love in history (Heyward 1989). This same sense of God as the power for wholeness and justice is expressed by Catherine Keller:

> If we meet God in ourselves, we meet her at the molten core of our heart's desire, ever again energising our courage and our quest (Keller 1986: 215).

Even more impersonally, but with no less degree of power, women theologians have been reclaiming images of God from the mystical tradition—God is light, fire, running water—as well as invoking images from the natural world—God as eagle, the Spirit as dove, swan, goose. So one of the issues to be tackled is: can the new re-imaging of God be consistent with tradition (Christianity and Judaism are meant here), or are we bursting the parameters and wineskins—and actually 'doing a new thing'?

If so, what status could our new imagining have for worshipping communities?

Can God as 'She' be prayed to and still be God as recognized by Christians? Does encountering God images as female make any difference to transforming the lives of poor women? These issues and many more I now tackle in Chapter 2.

Chapter Two

Encountering God as 'She'

> The end of patriarchal religion, which we are experiencing, has a liberating character only if it calls us into resistance. The question posed to organised religion is not how much the Father can be salvaged but how much power of resistance we can receive from God, the Ground of Life, and how long reform is still possible. At the end of the patriarchal era of religion, other images of God are emerging among us (Soelle 1995: 34).

We now enter hotly-disputed terrain. Before any real listening can take place, or an engaging with what could be the offering of a profound new experience of God, accusations of a new paganism are in the air, and the explorations of 'God as She' take on a semi-heretical hue. This was certainly the case in the notorious 'Re-imagining' Conference in the United States.[1] But is this also what happened when Julian of Norwich and Anselm of Canterbury spoke of Jesus as *our Mother*? When Hildegarde of Bingen preached on the Holy Spirit as the *greening power* dynamizing creation? Yet God, as Gerard Hughes has written, is always a *God of Surprises* (Hughes 1996). Surely that is the one aspect that we can be sure of in encountering God—namely, that we will be knocked off our feet, our breath taken away, our hearts burning within us, as the *mysterium tremendum et fascinans* (Otto 1958), the mystery which both captivates and yet holds us in awe and wonder, meets us—not on the holy mountain—but in the daily round of preparing food, caring for family, earning our living and paying attention to all our relationships.[2] Or maybe the mystery beckons, or is present to us not in the whirlwind (as in 1 Kgs 19), but in an intensity of awareness, or in a healing

1. See Beckman (1997).
2. I do not mean this to sound weak: *paying attention* to everything—from breathing, to a complexity of relations—is a high spiritual value. See Weil (1950); Murdoch (1970).

presence or a coming-to-peace with one's own body and life situation. As Kathy Galloway wrote so movingly,

> She comes with mother's kindnesses and bends to touch and heal.
> She gives her heart away in love for those who cannot feel (Galloway 1993: 39).

But why, 'She'? comes the cry. And the answer is complex. It is not only—as Chapter 1 hinted—that women have been excluded from imaging the divine (with the possible exception of Mary, Mother of Jesus—to whom we will return). It is partly the conviction that not to include female images leaves untouched the negative traditions on female bodiliness, the cumulative weight of negative—and totally unjustifiable—references to women as sewers, dirt, devil's gateways and so on. Even if it is retorted that these are negative traditions from which we have long moved on, there is still a strong dualistic residue. Culture is still seen as a male construction, and nature is imaged as female, as the inert, material background to be moulded (exploited?) in the service of human progress.[3] Even 'liberal' contemporary theologians have written that for culture to progress we need to leave behind the oceanic, female cosmic soup (Cobb 1981). The sense that sexuality and bodiliness are inferior to rationality and spirit dies hard, and still form the backcloth to enforced celibacy in the Roman Catholic Church. When I was a young idealistic mother of twenty-three, I read in the *Clergy Review* (now *Priest and People*), that 'marriage was an affair of babies crying in the night and the celibate priest was well out of it'! My reply was no doubt rose-tinted—at that stage I still had years of babies crying in the night to cope with! But the sense that all that is messy, irrational, unpredictable, chaotic and embarrassing about physicality must be identified with women, leaving 'clean' rationality for men, is still with us (despite Augustine's famous wrestling with embarrassing aspects of his own sexuality). Women have constantly been symbolized as bodily human nature, but it is a bodiliness negatively considered and imaged. The prime example of this would be the iconography of Mary of Magdala— in the West, at least (Haskins 1993). She, the (supposed) redeemed and forgiven prostitute carries the signal—even *your* poor flesh can be redeemed. (Yet the Eastern Church never forgot her mission to preach the Gospel and her role as *apostola apostolorum*—apostle of apostles.)

---

3. For the complex background to this see Merchant (1980, 1995). Also Rosaldo and Lamphere (1974).

Another figure, Hagar, the concubine of Abraham, holds powerful symbolic significance for the Latina American women and womanist theologians. Despite being cast off—twice—into the desert, devalued as slave, concubine and Egyptian, it was Hagar who was the first mother of a promised child, who received a revelation from God and who still lived (Gen. 16.13).

Thus, after an accumulation of negative images, the need for women to rediscover self-worth, the sense of being created in the image of God, to own a healed and healing bodiliness has fuelled much of the contemporary re-imagining.

But, it will be retorted, this is mere Freudian projection revisited, this time with a feminist hue! In response, let us consider what feminist theologians actually say. First, as I said earlier, many (but not all) writers stress the provisional nature of the imagery. The late and much-revered feminist theologian, Nelle Morton, in her essay 'The Goddess as Metaphoric Image' (Morton 1989), saw the imagery and what she called epiphany of the goddess as ushering in a new experience of the divine. She did not reify the goddess as such:

> When I speak of the Goddess as metaphoric image I am in no way refer-
> ring to an entity 'out there' who appears miraculously as a fairy god-
> mother and turns the pumpkin into a carriage. I am not even referring to
> a Goddess 'back there' as if I participate in resurrecting an ancient
> religion. In the sense that I am a woman I see the Goddess within myself.,
> but I see something more tangible, a concrete image or a concrete event,
> to capture my full attention to the present and draw me into the
> metaphoric process (Morton 1989: 110).

To use this new language of the female as divine can be a breakthrough to a new revelation. Similarly, Janet Morley (in discussion) has described her own experience of praying to God as Mother—initially an alien idea—as feeling as if the floodgates had been swept away. This has been the experience of many, myself included. Simply taking the risk of praying to God as Mother meant that suddenly a range of human (not only female) experiences were opened up and a process of healing was set in motion. It was not just that feelings of vulnerability, loss, of being misunderstood by those you love, stunned by failure, helpless in the face of the scale of tragedy, were met by a sense of God's presence to it all; it was that God somehow understood *female* human nature because it found *some home, some familiar place in God*. It is all right to have a female body. There is a goodness and a beauty—far from the degrading erotic forms paraded by culture—loved by God. Not only does God as female somehow respond to the awkwardness of coming to terms with our own female sexuality as being different; not only does she pose a challenge to ambiguous messages coming out of Christianity—that it is only all right to be an actively sexual female human being if you bear children (1 Tim. 2.16), or are a consecrated virgin; and the price to be paid for this in motherhood is considerable suffering and submission to one's husband—but we encounter her as giving a high value to the qualities so cherished by women, like compassion, empathy, relating, caring and nurturing, attention to the particular and embodied knowing. (This is not to fall into the trap of asserting that women are better than men in being compassionate and nurturing; nor to ignore the fact that many theologians are beginning to rate empathy and compassion highly; nor again to assign these qualities exclusively to women in an essentialist stereotyping [E. Farley 1996; Keen 1983]; but it is to say that women, because of role socialization, gender stereotyping, and because of long-rooted conviction that these qualities are crucial to human flourishing, have been carrying the torch in society for qualities and responsibilities which belong to the whole human race.)

This sense that praying and believing in God addressed in female imagery is a part of a process of actively moving towards God is frequently found in feminist writers. Mary Daly, in her ceaseless energy to provide an alternative to the armoury of male images of the divine, not only invokes the Goddess, but wrote of 'God the Verb':

> The naming of Be-ing as Verb—an intransitive verb that does not require an 'object'—expresses an Other way of understanding ultimate/intimate reality. The experience of many feminists continue to confirm that Naming be-ing as Verb is an essential leap in the cognitive/affective journey beyond patriarchal fixations (Daly 1973: xvii).

This suggestion that the activity of new naming is a dynamic process of discovery, strengthens Nelle Morton's belief that goddess metaphors usher in a new experience, *epiphany*, and revelation—but that as yet we are not quite there. The same idea is expressed by Carter Heyward, in that the word God implies a process,[4] a process of *godding*, that is, of *moving toward God*:

---

4. The influence of process theology is extensive for feminist theology. See Daly (1973)—and she is critical; Suchocki (1988), Keller (1986), Grey (1989), Christ (1997).

We god towards justice, moved by and moving the God-given voice by the
prophets, the God moving transpersonally through history, by us through
us (Heyward 1982: 153).

This process of moving towards new revelations of the Mystery of
God—in response to the needs of creation—is fully in keeping with the
promise of Christian and Jewish traditions and has been developed as
such by some feminist thinkers.[5] I now ask, how far can this actually
function—to name God 'She' and 'mother' and be understood as part of
traditional Christianity and Judaism?

Mining the Tradition

It has long been admitted that there is a fairly clear, if modest, strand
within Jewish tradition where God is imaged as female, as mother or
midwife.[6] Texts such as Isa. 42.14, 46.3-4, 66.13, speak of the tender
motherhood of God, crying out in labour, who at the same time does
not forget the child of her womb (Hos. 11.3-4; Isa. 49.15). Further,
God's compassionate love for her people, is rooted in womb-like love
(*rehem, rahamim*). This is developed by Phyllis Trible, as

> the journey of a metaphor from the wombs of women to the compassion
> of God… The allusion to the wombs of women carried in biblical words
> of divine mercy and compassion makes it clear that throughout the bible
> references to God who loves as a mother are more numerous than the
> number of explicit maternal images would suggest.[7]

It is this same theme of compassionate motherhood that Jesus echoes,
when he laments over Jerusalem, wanting to gather the people under his
wings, like the mother–hen her chickens (Mt. 23.37).[8]

For as has been mentioned, Jesus as mother is a theme movingly developed by both Anselm in the twelfth century and Julian of Norwich in
the thirteenth.[9] Anselm's prayer reads like a meditation on the Gospel
text:

---

5.   See, for example, Johnson (1994); Plaskow (1989); Lacugna (1993).
6.   See Hebblethwaite (1984).
7.   The reference to Phyllis Trible is Trible (1978) cited in Johnson (1994: 101).
8.   Paul also speaks of himself as both a nurse and a father to the community
(1 Thess. 2.7, 11–12).
9.   Interestingly, not by Hildegarde of Bingen.

And you, good Jesus, are you not also a mother?
Are you not a mother who like a hen gathers her chicks beneath her
wings?...
And you, my soul, dead in yourself, run under the wings of Jesus your
mother, and lament your griefs under his feathers.
Ask that your wounds may be healed and that, comforted, you may live
again.
Christ, my mother, you gather your chickens under your wings;
This dead chicken of yours puts himself under those wings...
Warm your chicken, give life to your dead one, justify your sinner.[10]

Julian of Norwich's theology of Jesus our Mother is developed in what
is called the *Long Text* of her visions or *Showings*. In the first place, Jesus
as our Mother is firmly placed within the context of the Trinity itself:

And so, in our making, God is our loving Father, and God all wisdom is
our loving Mother, with the love and the goodness of the Holy Spirit,
which is all one God, one Lord (Colledge and Walsh 1978: 58).

Secondly, it is also in the context of the incarnation, in the task of the
saving of the world that Christ is our Mother, bringing to birth the new
creation:

The second person of the Trinity is our mother in nature in our substan-
tial creation, in whom we are founded and rooted, and he is our Mother
of mercy in taking our sensuality...and by the power of his Passion, his
death and his Resurrection he unites to our substance (Colledge and
Walsh 1978: 58).

As Grace Jantzen remarks (1987: 116-24), Christ as our mother is pre-
pared to suffer more for us than are human mothers. He nourishes us—a
Eucharistic reference—and brings healing and comfort. Even if some
may feel this is an idealized picture of motherhood, focusing attention
away from the suffering reality of poor mothers, it is a crucially important image in linking the person of Christ, second person of the Holy
Trinity, with female bodily features in a positive and redemptive way.

A more contemporary example (see the examples in art referred to in
Chapter 1, p. 17) is the Christology of the US theologian, Mark Kline
Taylor, *Christus Mater* in his remarkable book, *Remembering Esperanza*
(Taylor 1993: 194-245).This is not so much a focus on the motherhood
of Christ as such, nor an emphasis on the suffering of mothers the world
over. *Christus Mater*, he tells us, is a constant reminder that matter *mat-
ters*; that we need Christology to be grounded in what he calls *mater-

10. Anselm cited in Johnson (1994: 150).

nalization. This involves two elements—first, the revaluing of women's reproductive powers, and secondly, the relocating of society's maternal functions. By this he means that it is no good calling for the revaluing of women's reproductive powers without undergoing a thoroughgoing social reform.[11] This means—as I see it—a real examination of the life-situation of mothers as carers right through a family's life-cycle. Not only the struggles with small children, but the increasing care for the elderly, the difficulties and humiliations experienced with gynaecological problems, the social position of widows and women in homes for the elderly who have lost all that made life worthwhile.[12] A Christic re-valuing would find its root, for example, in the attention which the earthly Jesus gave to the vulnerability of the small girl—the raising to life of Jairus's daughter—and the breaking of taboos around women with the flow of blood (Grey 1997b: 199-200).

With the theme of 'Jesus as our Mother' we seem to have moved far from God as Mother—and yet there is a vital connection. God moves in history as Jesus. There is even an implicit theology of Trinity here which could help to disentangle us from the all-male Trinity. For we see God's womb-like compassion for her children, revealed in Jesus, and lived out as embodied love in the praxis and lifestyle of Christic communities throughout history.

The Limits of the Symbol

Without wanting to diminish the beauty of this symbol and the strength, healing and comfort it increasingly brings (as well as the interfaith dimension it can encourage), there needs to be an element of caution. A symbol can become overloaded and we need to recognize its limits.

First, writers have alluded to the danger that an over-focus and stress on the motherhood of Jesus takes attention away from the vulnerable position of real mothers.[13] Real mothers who, in their poverty and pain

11. Here in Britain, for example, this means a focus on the poverty of single mothers; the fact that Britain has the greatest number of teenage pregnancies in the Europe; the poverty of Asian and Afro-Caribbean mothers, forced to take low-paid jobs at times inconvenient for their families; the women in prison without their babies; the suicidal depression of young mothers, and so on.

12. In Rajasthan, India, as part of the 'Wells for India' team, I have seen villages where there was not even a language for gynaecological problems. They were known as 'women's secret illnesses'.

13. Walker Bynum 1982; Newman 1995.

can never match up to Jesus our Mother. It is this lack of balance that I understand Mark Kline Taylor was trying to redress.

Secondly, the symbol, when used as the female equivalent of 'God the Father', can essentialize motherhood as the most elevated expression of being a woman.[14] Idealizing mothers directs attention away from the real situation of many mothers, poor and suffering, and from the fact that many women have had no choice in the matter. (This is in no way to underrate the importance of bearing and rearing children, these experiences can be the most meaningful and satisfying experiences of a woman's life: but they can also be the very opposite.)

It can also mask the fact that motherhood has been, and in many parts of the world still is, used as a means for the social control of women (Rich 1980). Life as a single woman is just not a viable option in these countries. The difference between First and Two Thirds' World here is immense. Women in the First World (or Northern hemisphere) will tend to give fewer years of their lives to child-rearing than their counterparts in the southern hemispheres, while many women from former communist countries were forced to work, and did not have a real option for child-rearing. Thus many women in the north are tending to see motherhood not as defining their entire identity, but as forming an important part of it. For women in the Two Thirds' World who have no access to contraception, and where the economic need for many children defines their reality, no other identity is possible.

Thirdly, the stereotype of mothers as nurturing and compassionate, and thus as sharing in the compassion of God the Mother, is only one dimension of being a mother. In many parts of the world it is qualities like strength, courage, initiative-taking and resistance which define the lives of mothers. In Jungian thought, mothers have been stereotyped as 'the Dark Mother, as devouring' (Becker 1973: 39–40; Wehr 1988: 111), and the young boy (sic!) is advised to break free of her, to attain a place in culture. The horror of bodiliness is made very plain here, and the projection of this onto the mother gives rise to the myth that women are more sexual than men and more 'close to nature'. But this is a far cry from the mothers of the Missing Ones, Mothers of the Plaza de Mayo, in Argentina, who lead the resistance and mourning for their missing husbands, sons and brothers, in great danger to their own lives; women who keep communities going in times of war and many situations where

14. And this, of course, happens in the Papal document, *Mulieris Dignitatem* 1988, of John Paul II.

women are both breadwinners, child-rearers and backbone to the community. I remember my mother's words at the death of my grandmother, who had been a war-widow with eight children to rear, on a widow's pension of 26 shillings a week: 'she was both father and mother to us'.

Fourthly, there is a tendency of some writers to make the Father symbol more acceptable by incorporating additional feminine traits within it. I think of Moltmann's 'motherly father' (Moltmann 1981). It need hardly be said that this fails to break the rigid hold and privileged status of masculine imagery for God. Nor does it help to solve the problem by allotting female identity to the Holy Spirit. As Mary Daly so famously quipped, 'He's female'. A range of writers from the tradition have attempted this, from the fourth-century Ephrem the Syrian to Leonardo Boff (Coakley 1988). But it just will not do! We are not looking for a neat arithmetical division of gender within the Godhead. Nor do we seek to carve up the Godhead in gender terms, believing that God's being is hidden in mystery, yet poured out and revealed to us in a richness of imagery, given for our healing and wholeness and to evoke our reverent love and right action.

So, concluding this section, I want to understand God imaged as Mother, that is, insisting that 'Mother' like 'Father' is a 'metaphor' for God—as a real enrichment of divine imagery, given for our healing, when understood in fluid, context-related interpretations. 'God as Mother' can also be developed within inclusive imagery for the Trinity, as well as in a rich theology of divine Wisdom, God as Sophia (Johnson 1994), to which I shall return.

But there is one whole area which challenges the above with a more fully fleshed out female imaginary. That is, God is not God, but *Goddess*; and it is on Thealogy, Theaphany that we now focus.[15]

Discovering the Goddess

Goddess religions are now flourishing in many countries. Her devotees include both women and men and it is clear that there are complex meanings involved in such enthusiasm. Nor can Goddess worship just be dismissed as New Age eclecticism, a passing trend, her devotees as eco-freaks, or as yearning for the exotic, although there can be elements of all of this in some forms of Goddess worship.

15. For an in-depth discussion on thealogy, see Raphael (1999), as part of this series.

Let me start with the certainties. First, it is absolutely clear that goddesses were worshipped in most ancient world religions and still are important in many Asian and African religions, as well as in the way new devotion to ancient goddesses is mushrooming (Spretnak 1982, Christ 1987, Matthews 1991). It is also known that among these, Earth mother goddesses held particular significance and were especially loved—Isis of Egypt, Inanna of Sumer, Astarte of Babylon, Asherah in Canaan, Demeter of Greece, the Hindu Durga, Pachamama of Mexico, and Ceridwen, beloved of Celtic myth being some of these. What remains ambiguous is the status of women and the nature of relations between men and women when the Goddesses held power.

There is a popular theory sustaining much of the enthusiasm of Goddess-worship, namely, that before patriarchy became rigidly established (generally assumed to be around 600 BCE) and enshrined inflexible law-codes which fixed the subordination of women in society,[16] there was a Golden Age of matriarchy in which the Goddess reigned supreme over a biophilic culture in which there was harmony between women and men, and consequently women's authority and role in society were significant and respected. In a world where ecological disaster threatens, this theory appeals to a nostalgia in many people for a lost paradise, an unspoilt garden of harmonious relations between all species. Whether this is seen as the biblical Garden of Eden, lost through sin, the egalitarian paradise of the Goddess, or the psychoanalytic yearning for the lost mother, these impulses combine to suggest that the victory of militarism, the overwhelming violent character of our society have prompted the return of the Goddess (Whitmont 1980), or even the *rebirth* of the Goddess (Christ 1997), the re-awakening of the Old Religion, as the only hope for a sustainable future.

The main reason for questioning the Golden Age of the Goddess is the lack of historical evidence (Binford 1982; Ruether 1992: 144-65). Rosemary Ruether, in an earlier work (1983: 47-61) presumed an early goddess figure in many religions (as in Sumer and Babylonia), who is eventually displaced by her consort/son. Among other sources she builds on the myth of the Earth Mother Tiamat, slain by her son Marduk, who then creates the earth from his mother's body (Ruether 1983: 50-53). Another ancient mythic pattern is the marriage of the Goddess with the priest-king (or dying-rising god-king). Changing patterns of gods and

16. For example, the Babylonian code of Hammurabi, the Hebraic Law Codes, the sixth-century Athenian codes of Solon, the sixth-century Hindu code of Manu.

goddesses, she writes, reflect the development from older forms of society where there was a more direct dependency on spontaneous natural powers:

> In the new world of cities and agriculture, an emerging élite owns both the land and the labor of peasants and slaves... An aristocratic and sacerdotal ruling class, both male and female, cooperate in this new system of urban and agricultural order. The image of the divine comes primarily from the characteristics of this ruling class: god or goddess is seen in the image of sovereign power (Ruether 1983: 49).

However, Ruether argues that we cannot deduce from the fact that when the goddesses were worshipped, societies took the egalitarian patterns that we would hope. This is to project feminist wishful thinking backwards with the kind of nostalgia that many Christians project onto a pre-lapsarian Garden of Eden! More helpful, in her view, is to trace the matricentric and matrifocal patterns in such societies—and her studies are cross-cultural—and to understand why the meaningful, authoritative role of women was lost, as the predominance of men took over and patriarchy became established in law. The interesting conclusion of Ruether—which has such relevance for today—is that many matricentric societies and cultural groupings failed to provide a meaningful role for men, who were thrown back in to making warfare and other forms of violence (including violence to and subjection of their own women) their peculiarly masculine role (Ruether 1992: 163-72).[17] Quoting Peggy Reeve Sanday, she writes:

> Sanday suggests that, under environmental stress, scapegoating of women is accentuated in those societies that already have conflictual patterns; that is, where male resentment of female maternity has not been successfully balanced by adult male cultural roles (Ruether 1992: 169).

If this is true in the past, there are important lessons to be learnt for the present.

Other writers—notably the late Maria Gimbutas and Asphodel Long—argue that Goddess worship lingered on even under patriarchy (Gimbutas 1989, 1989a; Long 1992).[18] In the context of the ancient

---

17. This is a fascinating subject. It is beyond my present study, except insofar as it throws light on the resistance of the imaging of God as female because it seems to exclude men.

18. They are writing about Europe: clearly in Asia, Africa this is indisputable. There are also traces of the indigenous goddesses in Latin American cultures.

faith of Israel, Asphodel Long's challenging book *In a Chariot Drawn by Lions* traces the struggle of Yahwism in Israel to establish itself in the face of the loyalty of the people to the older goddess Asherah (or Astarte), worshipped in grove and even in the temple. In the often hysterical reaction to the goddess, to paganism, and to female sexuality seen in the prophets of Israel, lurks the spectre of *otherness* (Plaskow 1990: 148-50).

An increasingly popular area of goddess worship today connected with the devotion to the ancient goddesses, is the way that feminist Jungian thinkers have seen in the goddess principle the affirmation of female bodiliness, the 'feminine principle', 'the transformation mysteries of femaleness', the process of being 'initiated into womanhood'. These writers, for example Naomi Goldenberg and Christine Downing, are interested in the way Jungian archetypes nurture the growth of the female psyche. The area is fraught with pitfalls, based as it is around Jung's idea of two personality types, *animus,* a masculine core of psychic capacities, and *anima,* a complementary feminine one. Although Jung was keen that both men and women, in their quest for psychic integration, developed both sides of their personality into an androgynous whole, yet he was insensitive to the fact that he retained an essentialist, complementary view of what is masculine and what is feminine.

Nonetheless, archetypal images are used by feminists to nurture growth, 'for images provide a knowledge that we can interiorise rather than apply, can take to that place in ourselves where there is water and where reeds and grasses grow'[19] (Downing 1989: 119). Christine Downing relates how she was helped by the goddess Artemis, 'The Lady of Wild Things', at a particular juncture of her life. Here she shows how vital it is for women to be nurtured psychically by female images of the divine:

> To be fed only male images of the divine is to be badly malnourished. We are starved for images that recognise the sacredness of the feminine and the complexity of the richness, and nurturing power of female energy. We hunger for images of human creativity and love inspired by the capacity of female bodies to give birth and nourish, for images of how humankind participates in the natural world suggested by reflection on the correspondences between menstrual rhythms and the moon's waxing and waning. We seek images that affirm that the love women receive

---

19. Demaris Wehr, recognizing that despite all difficulties, women have been helped by archetypal images, has tackled the problems inherent in their use in her helpful study (Wehr 1988).

from women, from mother, sister, daughter, lover, friend, reaches as deep
and is trustworthy, necessary and sustaining as is the love symbolised by
father, brother, son or husband (Downing 1989: 120-21).

This use of goddess imagery for the growth and nurturing of the female
psyche is taken a stage further, as an organized community life-style by
the Wicca movement (a branch of the many neo-paganism movements)
of which the American witch, Starhawk, is a well-known exponent.[20]
Again, closeness to the earth and its rhythms personified by the Goddess,
and embodied in rituals in her honour, is the focus. On the basis of this
Starhawk has constructed ethical values, and works for peace and
ecological harmony in many ways (Starhawk 1989).

Many of these elements are contained in the work of Carol Christ[21]
whose life can be described an as *Odyssey with the Goddess*, the title of
one her recent books (Christ 1995). In her early work on literature
(Christ 1980), she was searching for female images to nurture women on
their spiritual quest. In her article 'Why Women Need the Goddess'
(Christ 1979)—still regarded as inspirational—she had pleaded for a
female principle of the divine. But after her dramatic personal discovery
of the Goddess she renounced her tenured professorship and went to
live on the island of Lesbos, as she relates in her latest book (Christ
1997). Not only has she written personally on the transformation in her
own life in the course of this long odyssey—and there have been many
pitfalls and struggles—but she has also struggled to construct a
philosophy of the goddess movement.

Conscious that destructive alienation from earth and nature are built
into modern identity, Christ tries to heal this separation through relationship with the Goddess. But in doing so she blurs the distinctions
between the Goddess as metaphor for nature and the living earth, the
divine female principle, and the goddess as reality. Using some ideas
from process theology[22] (but without the technical structures or developing these at all), the Goddess has now become the web of life and the

20. Wicca is controversial for many reasons, its link with magic and witchcraft in
particular. But it is not clear whether it is a new religion or a re-creation of the old
goddess religion, and how feminist it is. It also increasingly borrows elements from
other non-Western goddess religions (see Eller 1996: 314).

21. See the forthcoming PhD thesis of Ruth Mantin, University of Southampton
entitled 'Goddess Spirituality and Female Identity'.

22. Process theology is developed from the thought of Alfred North Whitehead
(1924), and Charles Hartshorne (1948).

interconnectedness of all things (Christ 1997: 113-34). In reconnecting with the earth, she follows, among others, the inspiration of Susan Griffin:

> I know I am made from this earth, as my mother's hands were made from this earth, as her dreams were made from this earth, and all I know, I know in this earth, the body of the bird, this pen, this paper, these hands, this tongue speaking, all that I know speaks to me through this earth and I long to tell you, you who are earth too, and listen as we speak to each other of what we know: the light is in us (Griffin 1978: 227).

The Goddess as the interconnectedness of all things, holds us in interdependent relation with each other and with the earth, and within her diversity flourishes. So, according to Christ, the dilemma of the One and the Many is solved, and the Goddess appears in a multiplicity of forms. (Christ is rightly sensitive to the fact that she only deals with European Goddesses.) To embrace the Goddess as the living web of life enables us to alter our views on death, life after death and tragedy. We will no longer hold onto immortality as our birthright because the Goddess has taught us how to respect the seasons of giving birth and dying. Though we will not cease to grieve, or feel anger and pain at loss and failure, we do not need to accept what she calls the 'tragic view of life' that patriarchy has instilled into us. We take a long view of things when it comes to the survival of the species (Christ 1997: 127).

Though I find these views on evil and tragedy unconvincing—because they fail to take an active stance of resistance to global injustice—it is time now to ask what is helpful about the range of approaches to the goddess images which have been presented.

The first attraction is that women—and any person—who have suffered oppression under patriarchy are brought into a completely new space where the female body, bodily rhythms and sexuality are valued. We cannot underestimate the healing value of rituals focusing on reverencing female bodies which religious traditions have vilified and despised at worst, and controlled and tolerated at best.

Secondly, connected with this is that care and attention are given to all aspects of nature, her rhythms and settings, the qualities of pebbles, rocks, flowing water, light, birds, colour, seasonal variety, diversity of the creatures. Thus an ethic of care and responsibility for creation is manifested by, for example, vegetarianism and care for animals, protection and planting of trees and protests against new roads, and in a multitude of ways working for a sustainable lifestyle.

It would be easy to criticize the goddess movement for some of the excesses of her devotees. For example, it solves nothing if, instead of glorifying the male principle, we now glorify the female; if, instead of political action, we focus on self-indulgent rituals affirming female sexuality; or, instead of demonizing paganism (as in early Christianity), we turn it on its head and make it our preferred principle. Not all that went on in pagan religions was without blame. Rather, we should ask what are the challenges to be taken seriously.

And clearly, one of the important issues is that if the reason for the suppression of these earth-based, goddess-based spiritualities was the reverencing of the female and the world of the female, it is simply not adequate for Christianity to reject all forms of neo-paganism without responding to the need for a female imaginary within her own spirituality and faith practice. Simply heaping divine attributes on Mary of Nazareth, the mother of Jesus, does not solve the problem. Since Augustine, women have been held to symbolize the body, a carnality prohibiting spiritual development: many aspects of the goddess movement are pointing away back to re-valuing this body.

Secondly, there is a long tradition of calling the earth and nature 'our mother'. In so doing connections are made with earth-based spiritualities of indigenous peoples. We are also re-connecting with the material base of all our living and loving—but without necessarily falling into making of nature a divine principle or forgetting that the Mystery of Life we call God/God/ess is always named symbolically and metaphorically. All that we see and love in this universe is within the Mystery—which is so much more than we see and love. What Carol Christ has expressed through the *metaphor* of Goddess as web of life, is what all the great Christian writers have been trying to express through the ages. And the test of metaphors for God is not only their correspondence with tradition, but their success or failure in inspiring new and juster modes of living. As Ruether has pointed out, if the Goddess movements have no adequate role for men, they will fail. If they take a quiescent attitude to the global need for structural justice, concentrating on the healing of individual women, they will fail. And if they take an arbitrary attitude to historical truth, blurring the boundaries between civilizations geared to the public worship of ancient goddesses and the role of these goddesses as purely psychic images today, they lose credibility.

But one of the crucial issues raised by this exploration has been that of diversity and otherness. Was the Goddess banished because she was *other*? I now explore this in the context of Judaism and the goddess. It will raise for us the way in which feminist images of the divine encounter the question of ambiguity in God.

Chapter Three

Images of God in Jewish Feminism

Shekinah
calling us
from exile
inside us exiled
calling us
home
home
(Gottlieb 1982).[1]

Shekinah, a Hebrew word for God's presence, is often described as a special female way of God being present. Thus, Virginia Mollenkott writes:

> The Shekinah glory of God, that feminine presence, dwelt in the Temple
> of Jerusalem; but John 1.14 together with John 2.21 asserts that the Body
> of Christ has now become the temple and is the perfect dwelling-place of
> the Shekinah glory… In other words the presence of Christ the Shekinah
> within the worshipping congregation, is expected to expose the classist,
> racist and sexist prejudices (Mollenkott 1983: 40, also cited in Kellenbach
> 1994: 128).

But this citation illustrates in one fell swoop how Christian feminist
writers can appropriate distinctive Jewish images and give them an
assumed Christian fulfilment. Christian feminism is itself not free from
anti-Judaism (Kellenbach 1994). This chapter therefore focuses mainly

---

1. Every effort has been made to trace the copyright owner without success.
Anyone claiming copyright should contact Sheffield Academic Press.
   Even though there are two other books in this series, (1) *Feminist Judaism*, and (2)
A Feminist Reading of the Hebrew Scriptures, it is crucial in this conversation about the
'new naming' of God for this book also to engage seriously with Jewish feminism as
discussion and dialogue partner in what must count as the most important area of
theology, the attempt to name the transcendent mystery of the divine.

on some of the efforts within feminist Judaism itself towards the naming of God.

There are both similarities and differences from Christian feminism in the way that Jewish feminists are struggling towards this new naming of the Sacred. One of the similarities is the struggle to move beyond the rigid monotheism of Yahweh, imaged as male:

> God's maleness is so deeply and firmly established as part of the Jewish conception of God that it is almost difficult to document: it is simply part of the lenses through which God is seen. Maleness is not a distinct attribute, separable from God's anger or mercy or justice. Rather it is expressed through the total picture of God in Jewish texts and liturgy (Plaskow 1990: 123).

Again, a similar link is made between a male, dominating God and a male-dominated society in which women are 'other' and treated as inferior other, with no rights in law to inherit property.[2] So, simply to highlight the incidence of female images of God—numerically few, as was seen in Chapter 1—which contrast with more frequent images of God as judge, king and ruler, offering the alternative of God as midwife, mother, birthgiving parent, or even the image of God's *Shekinah* as life-giving presence, does little to shake this dominant picture. God is simply male with a few feminine attributes (like the 'motherly father' mentioned above). Nonetheless, as with Christian feminism, the process of new naming began—according to Rita Gross—with the recovery of distinctively feminine imagery for the divine (Gross 1979), while recognizing that even these female attributes are firmly embedded in a patriarchal context.

The second suggestion of Rita Gross is to incorporate female religious symbols from a non-Western context into an identifiable Jewish concept of God. Learning from Goddesses such as Kali, Lakshmi and Durga is suggested as means of re-imaging the Hebrew God (Gross 1978). But the problem with this, apart from the difficulty of making comparisons between one culture and another, is the actual history within Judaism of the Hebrew Goddess and the way she has been used by patriarchal religion to symbolize women negatively. The very history of the suppression of the Goddess has also been a source of anti-Judaism even in

---

2.   Judith Plaskow in another article (1982) maintains that *halacha* (Jewish law) 'is itself a product of Judaism's deep-seated view of women as other, reinforced though a theology that continues to image God as exclusively male' (Umansky 1989: 190).

feminist theology, where there has been an uncritical blaming of Judaism for the death of the Goddess (Plaskow 1991: 103). As she writes:

> It seems that in this case, as with the image of the wrathful God, it is easier for Christian feminists to point the finger at problematic aspects of the Christian tradition as they also appear within Judaism than to deal with them in Christianity itself (Plaskow 1982).

Even though Judaism would come to forbid Goddess worship, she continues, the exclusive worship of Yahweh should be seen against the background in ancient near-Eastern cultures of an ancient struggle between Goddess-centred, matrifocal societies and emergent patriarchal societies with their ascendant male gods.

But the recovery of the lost Hebrew goddess is only one approach. Other possibilities are offered. One would be to keep the word *Elah*, goddess, meaning not *Elilah*, female idol, 'a false naming', but as 'God'—the difficulty being that for the majority '*Elah*' will still be seen as other to the Hebrew God. Another path is taken by Lynn Gottlieb, Rabbi and storyteller. She retains the traditional words, but re-images, re-translates and explores new meanings:

> Lynn Gottlieb's new namings of God are performance pieces, written/ spoken in a dramatic, incantatory style, and drawing together the imagined resources of a number of religious traditions. Her 'A Psalm' for example, moves behind the Biblical psalms to their ancient Near Eastern precursors, drawing on the Babylonian hymn to Ishtar to sing in praise of God. Images from the original hymn are combined with many names for God from the Jewish tradition, yielding a litany of names and images that evoke the infinite, changing and flowing depths of God's nature:
> PRAISE HER
> MOST AWESOME OF THE MIGHTY
> REVERE HER
> SHE IS A WOMAN OF THE PEOPLE (Plaskow 1990: 141).

Yet another way forward is taken by Marcia Falk in her work on new blessings for rituals (1989a). It is in her work that the important idea is encountered that an 'authentic monotheism is not a singularity of image, but an embracing *unity of multiplicity* of many images' (129). This notion—embedded in the idea of the 'endless unfolding of God'—is becoming increasingly influential in both Jewish and Christian feminist circles. (It is developed, for example, by Sallie McFague, through her metaphors of God as Mother, Lover, Friend and the idea of the world as the *Body of God*.) Thus Judith Plaskow also introduces images of God as lover, friend, companion and co-creator—all images familiar to the

Jewish tradition. Falk, in her attempt to 'shatter the idolatrous reign of the lord/God/king', creates and uses new images, such as 'well-spring or source of life',[3] 'fountain, or flow of our lives'.[4] This is part of her attempt to create a theology of divine immanence (Falk 1989: 55).

But, the holiness of God as present to the whole of creation is also a key motif for Jewish faith—as is seen by the (already-cited) image of *Shekinah*:[5] so the holiness of God is manifested also as fountain, ground and source, wellspring, place, rock, ground—images also found in the later Christian mystical tradition. What Judaism calls the *unity of multiplicity* of images is both suggestive of the inexhaustible depth of God; but also introduces the idea that it is not monotheism which is the problem but our interpretation of it as intrinsically male and dominating. At the same time many feminist writers stress the diversity of these images and are slower to impose a too-hastily assumed unity.

Re-enter the Goddess

But before this is discussed, the question of the goddess re-enters. As the previous chapter related, images of the Hebrew/Canaanite/Babylonian goddess remained within the consciousness, memory and loyalty of the Jewish people for a long period (Raphael Patai [1967], Elinor Gadon [1989], Asphodel Long [1992]). It has even been that monotheism/Yahwism was established much later than had been thought. The presence of statues of Asherah in the temple hint that the Hebrew/Canaanite goddess at least co-existed with Yahwism for a period, and possibly she was thought of as Yahweh's consort:

> Certainly the presence of an Asherah in the Temple for much of its existence suggests that Israelites were hardly indifferent to goddesses. Rather, it seems that, despite prophetic invective and theology, for a good span of history, Yahweh was popularly regarded as having a consort (Plaskow 1990: 148).

The well-known denunciations of the prophet Jeremiah (7.18; 44.25) against the women and men who were baking cakes for the Queen of Heaven, Elijah's fulminations against Baal ending with Yahweh's re-

3.   *Eyn ha-khayyim.*
4.   *Nishmat kol khai.*
5.   Marcia Falk gives a word of caution: *Shekinah*, she says, as the immanent presence of God is often considered as secondary to the transcendence of God: both needed to be re-configured.

sounding victory and the subsequent denigration of Ahab's Queen
Jezebel throughout history (1 Kgs 21), Hosea's imaging of God's relationship with Israel as the husband abandoned by his prostitute wife who
tenderly woos her back again (Hos. 2), this very multiplicity of images
combines to symbolize female sexuality and goddesses negatively. As
Judith Plaskow puts it:

> Anxiety about polytheism, sensuousness, female imagery and goddesses
> tend to get lumped together both with each other and the general oppro-
> brium the term paganism arouses (1990: 149).

The argument can be pushed further. When we take the cumulative
weight of negative imagery—the use of the Hosea image throughout history, where the husband is always faithful, the wife always the whoring
prostitute—together with the Western Christian symbolizing of Mary
Magdalen as repentant prostitute, and the reversing of the bad sexuality
of Eve through the good sexuality of Mary of Nazareth, expressed as
virginal motherhood, the resistance to the goddess is seen to be intrinsically bound up with the resistance to negative female imagery as such.
And if the parameters of new naming or re-naming of God are to be
bounded by what is actually possible (practically and theologically) in
both historical Jewish and Christian communities, then there are limits
to including Goddess imagery. But that must not prevent understanding
that the rejection of the Goddess and the vilifying of paganism as such,
has as much to do with patriarchy's self-understanding, its fear of what is
chaotic, irrational, beyond control, sexual, dis-ordered, and the projection of all this as female. Paganism in its original meaning is the religion
of country-dwellers, as opposed to the cities. But the Goddess in a patriarchal world, instead of symbolizing the divine counterpart of her consort, has come to encapsulate both the *idealized and loathed shadow side of
the norm of being human*.

Hence, woman as 'other', has summed up many of these irrational
fears, fears that surface time and time again when the rigidity and order
of the patriarchal legal system is disturbed, and repressive action is called
for. Thus the Great European Witch Hunt focused more on single
women, than the married or those controlled within cloisters. Today the
vilification of single woman parents presents a new form of scapegoat-
ing: the 'good woman'—wife and mother—is again identified with the
nurture of children and husband; while single mothers are accused of
sexual promiscuity, scrounging on the government's benefit system and
various forms of irresponsibility.

Embracing the Other as *Beloved*?

How we understand 'otherness' is crucial for the new naming of God. I have mentioned one form of 'otherness' grappled with in both Judaism and Christianity—women as 'other' to the monotheism that undergirds the foundations of both religions and the communities in which they struggle. Another form of 'otherness' is the way Christians have treated Jews as 'other', specifically in the way European Christendom has been constructed on the exclusion of and discrimination against both Jews and Muslims. Because this exclusion was expressed in such extreme forms, from vilification in language, regular pogroms and expulsions, the death camps of Auschwitz as part of Hitler's 'final solution', to the more recent ethnic cleansing of the wars in the Balkans, it is impossible to use words like the 'otherness' of God, without recognizing the horrific consequences of the Christian acting out of this understanding of 'otherness', and its link with dominant power structures. My own intuition is to hold in tension 'otherness' with the ethical call to establish connection-in-justice together with the political call to build solidarity.

Nor, as I have said, are feminist theologians innocent of anti-Judaism in these respects (Plaskow 1991, Brock 1988, Kellenbach 1994). There are two specific areas involved here. The first is that the reaction of some feminists to the discovery of the goddesses of the ancient Near East, and the awareness that an event that has been called a 'cosmic matricide'[6] lies behind the death of the goddess and the triumph of Yahwism, has been one of blaming Judaism. Yet, as we have just seen, Judith Plaskow explained the death of the goddess as a much wider phenomenon affecting the whole of the ancient Near East.

The second area is in Christian feminist Christology. Unwittingly, in their efforts to construct a liberating, inclusive Christology, feminist theologians have also been accused of elevating—however unintentionally—the uniqueness of Jesus overagainst Judaism. Here again, Judith Plaskow insists that the Jesus movement must be seen against the background

---

6.   As Catherine Keller has written: 'The matricide, we begin to realise, constitutes the central act of the heroic life-style, the ritual gesture in which the patriarchal ego must participate at every moment—at *this* very moment. "The combat, the victory and the Creation" constitute the theological psychology of the west. The covert slaughter of the mother is this culture's bond of re-enactment' (Keller 1986: 78).

of reform movements within Judaism.[7]

Hence the urgency in Jewish–Christian feminist discussion is to affirm the 'otherness' of the Jewish feminist process of re-envisioning the God of Judaism and to resist all attempts to collapse the one process into the other. The other ethical task for Christian feminists is to examine our own complicity in language where Jewish women have appeared as 'other' in a negative interpretation. One area, for example, is to challenge the stereotypes of Jewish women in Western literature (Bitton-Jackson 1982).

But the crucial, unavoidable area of 'otherness' is the sense in which God is other, and irreducibly other. This 'otherness' cannot be collapsed into human terms, or encapsulated by any anthropomorphic imagery, however inclusive and all-embracing these images may appear. The 'otherness' of God has been criticized constantly so far in this book in the sense of God as 'dominating other', and as such, legitimizing oppressive social relations. I have also spoken of woman or other social groups as 'other', different in the sense of the 'despised other'. Judith Plaskow writes of feminist theology's attempt to name God in what has been rejected:

> In imaging God as female, as darkness, as nature, and as a myriad of other metaphors taken from realms devalued and spurned, we re-examine and value the many forms of Otherness, claiming their multiform particularity as significant and sacred (Plaskow 1990: 167).

The Jewish faith has many images of the otherness of God. I recall immediately the sense that the love of God is far more compassionate and faithful than human love. Isaiah wrote that even if the mother forsake her sucking child, yet God would not forsake God's people (Isa. 49.15). God, in contrast with human beings, will not take revenge:

> I will not execute my fierce anger;
> I will not again destroy Ephraim;
> for I am God and not mortal,
> the Holy One in your midst,
> And I will not come in wrath (Hos. 11.9).

But this compassionate, peace-loving and sustaining God is 'other' in what I would call 'acceptable otherness'. Yet there are still more problematic elements, where God seems close to the terrifying and destruc-

---

7.   For the most thorough study of Christian feminism anti-Judaism, see Kellenbach (1994).

tive aspects of life. Jacob wrestles with God and comes away with a limp. Moses cannot behold the face of God. Cities are destroyed by the wrath of God. Much of our naming of God has shrunk from grappling with a God responsible for the totality of existence. As Isaiah wrote:

> I form light and create darkness, I make weal and create woe.
> I the Lord do all these things (Isa. 45.7).

Christianity has shrunk from tackling the question of God and evil and facing uncomfortable answers. In asserting that God is a God of love, Christian theology has always argued that evil has no part in God: it is then forced into endlessly constructing theodicies to defend God in the face of evil. But, if God is indeed Creator—a firm belief of both Judaism and Christianity—it could be that Judaism is more faithful to this insight by not removing all attributes of God which seem to conflict with divine Goodness. Sadly, Christianity has made this a yardstick of its anti-Judaist theology—to hold up the 'Old Testament God of wrath' as the shadow side of the 'Christian God of love'.

But it could be that female imagery offers a way forward. Since the female has come to symbolize many of the terror-creating, disordered, uncontrollable elements of creation—and this is clear, for example, in the symbolism of the Hindu goddess Kali—could this be a possible way to reclaim certain aspects of creation as God-given and worthy of reverence? Instead of refusing to name God as a God of power and might—where power and might seem to legitimize military force as God-ordained—could sexuality as a powerful form of loving be honoured? And find its source in God? Could the power and authority of mothers be honoured—and be seen to image God's authority? Female decision-making and judgment could equally be seen as worthy of respect.

The problem with this way forward is that it seems like essentialism in another guise: why should women symbolize sexuality, when both men and women are sexual beings? The other problem is that there are terrifying aspects of creation—violence in all forms and 'natural' disasters, to name but two—and many people fear that to name God as responsible for everything (including evil), undermines faith in God's goodness and love.

Yet Jewish faith gives us two limits to the otherness of God. While insisting that God is inexhaustible mystery (and the feminist naming— as we have seen—insists also on God's nearness and immanence), Judaism has a powerful tradition of God's holiness and God's justice. What Jewish feminism seems to be saying is that God's holiness can also be seen in surprising places—in the holiness and vulnerability of giving birth, in the female body, in the prophetic authority and courageous leadership of women. God is also revealed in a passion for justice, and in this case God's passion is for the most vulnerable, weak and rejected. It is not merely that God's passion is for justice for women (and all vulnerable groups). It is that the activity of justice-making is what defines authentic community. For the new naming of God is not an arbitrary, individualistic task. It is not a question of what images have an aesthetic appeal to an individual, but what images call into being authentic forms of community and just expressions of society.

The feminist privileging of the ethical search for justice and healing, of self and community, is the binding element in the process of new naming, the creation of blessings, the connection with Jewish tradition, and the attempt to re-envision Jewish monotheism cleansed of all its patriarchal and destructive trappings.

So, with a proper respect for contextual differences, and mindful of the difficulties encountered in this chapter, I now look deeper, for this search for God as our passion for justice, a search embarked upon by diverse groups of religious feminists.[8]

8. It is to be expected that there will be commonalities in this feminist new naming of God. Seeking justice is a common starting point. Sensitivity to difference, to configurations of power and to cross-fertilizations will be sought.

Chapter Four

God—Our Passion for Justice

Terrified, we see. It is terrible, what we see. And it is good that we see together that we are not alone. We see broken body-selves trying to be healed; separated people yearning for relation; suffering humanity, raging for justice; nations, strangers, spouses, friends, lovers, lovers, children, sisters, brothers with us, we begin to remember ourselves, compelled by a power in relation that is relentless in its determination to break down the boundaries and boxes that separate us. We are driven to speak the Word that spills among us:

'Without our touching, there is no God'.

'Without our relation, there is no God'.

Without our crying, our yearning, our raging, there is no God. For in the beginning is the relation, and in the relation is the power that creates the world through us, and with us, and by us, you and I, you and we, and none of us alone (Heyward 1982: 171-72).

There can hardly be an image or metaphor of God emerging from Christian feminism which has more global appeal than this, God as *our passion for justice,* especially in communities whose organizing focus is the struggle for freedom. This is as true of women's movements from Latin America, Africa and Asia as of justice-seeking groups in Europe and North America. There are obvious connections here with the orienting focus of a diversity of liberation theologies. Nor does it mean that God imaged as passion for justice is always invoked in impersonal terms, or exclusive of the images presented already. God as nurturing mother, as sister, friend, companion and lover, *is* the God who empowers us to make justice. It seems that it is the very experienced static-ness of the traditional images of God which have called forth this dynamic image of a God who not only 'hears the cries of the poor' (Ps. 72.12-14), but whose compassion and active solidarity transform the unjust situation. Out of the depths of poverty, landlessness, racial and sexual discrimination, comes a great cry of anguish—but a cry of deep faith, that God is with the struggle. And that God will be effective in redeeming and transforming the injustice.

So this is the first point, that the God who is passion for justice arises not from an abstract concept of God, speculation, a new system or theory which neatly fits new situations (as if injustice is not as ancient as society), but from the concrete experience of struggle. *Discovering God is enacting God.*[1] I argue in this chapter, that God as 'our passion for justice' pushes forward the naming of God in a new and creative way and leads to a revelation of God as compassionate with our suffering and suffering with us. Within this process of new naming will be seen a response to the critique of theologians such as Edward Farley, who are inclined to dismiss what they call 'praxis theologies' (theologies committed to social transformation) as merely useful, but lacking in theological depth. Thus Farley writes:

> their attempt [i.e. that of praxis theologies] to support a constituency's struggle by means of a new iconography appears to constitute an independent and exclusive way to the question of God (E. Farley 1996: 16).

However, he continues, these praxis theologies omit certain important tasks in a theology of God. First, they simply *assume* that their narrative is a theology of God without indicating what justifies one iconography over another. Secondly, he argues that the methods of justifying imagery—either reclaiming marginalized biblical imageries, or using political efficacy as self-justifying (both of which are relevant to Christian feminism)—are inadequate, even if presenting a certain level of plausibility. For invoking social transformation masks a kind of projectionism and a pragmatism. Both arguments appear to invoke God as merely socially useful (E. Farley 1996: 16-17).[2]

---

1.   See Grigg (1994) who argues that this motif, *enacting the divine*, is typical of the thinking about God of feminist theology.

2.   E. Farley 1996: 16-17: 'The reason for saying God is just and loving is the efficacy of this imagery in social transformation. Perhaps so. But what we have here is a reversed Marxism, and where there is Karl Marx, Ludwig Feuerbach is not far behind. For Marx, God-language functions to legitimate social systems. Praxis theologies would replace iconographies of oppressive legitimisation with a liberating iconography… Pragmatism offers a way to retain human values and human transformative agendas while acknowledging the historical, plural and relative character of human experience. At the same time, pragmatism can be a foil for Feuerbach, a reduction of religious reality to human usages, a divine imagery without God.'

What kind of force should this criticism have? It would be irresponsible to disregard these remarks, as they issue, not from the kind of abstract theology that feminist theology resists, but from a desire to understand the images of God emerging from what Farley calls the 'facticity of redemption', the dynamics of the redeeming situation, whether personal, inter-human or social. And yet, in the conclusion to his work, Farley admits:

> This theology of God has said little about the specific struggles of embattled and victimised minorities, women, or poor people. These struggles are, needless to say, the concrete context of theology and therefore the theology of God. *This situation of subjugated victims is where theology begins* as it attests to the possibility and facticity of redemptive transformation (E. Farley 1996: 314, my italics).

But, if 'the situation of subjugated victims' is really where theology begins, why are the claims of 'praxis theologies' not taken more seriously? So, mindful of Farley's earlier warning that God not be reduced to merely a question of social usefulness, I respond by showing that this is exactly where feminist liberation theologians do begin, not only in the struggle for full humanity,[3] but in the actual experience of the power and redeeming agency of God in the process of transformation. I also show that in the struggles of many writers, 'transformation' is not a category restricted solely to political change: it is as much about personal and inter-human redemption as well as including the flourishing of the entire earth community. I first take as inspirational for Euro-American feminism the work of Carter Heyward; I then explore the different ways the picturing of God as source and power of justice-making works in the theology of Latina and Mujerista theology and show how this imaging is intrinsically focused on the compassion of God, ending by seeing compassion as a power for transformation even when faced with the tragic dimensions of existence.

The Inspiration of Carter Heyward

Carter Heyward, whose whole work is inspired by the image of God as *passion for relation*, or *passion for justice*, or *power in relation*, rejected such

3. See Ruether (1983: 19): 'Theologically speaking, whatever diminishes or denies the full humanity of women must be presumed not to reflect the divine, or to reflect the authentic nature of things, or to be the message or work of an authentic redeemer or a community of redemption.'

traditional images as the faraway, unchanging God as

> a distant controlling device, manufactured in the minds of men who have
> bent themselves low before ideals of changeless Truth, deathless Life, pure
> spirit, perfect reason, and other qualities associated with the changeless
> God (Heyward 1982: 7).

Though this quotation has a slight feel of a caricature, nonetheless it
refers accurately to one version of classical theism[4]. Heyward's method,
as with many other feminist theologians, is to rise above dualistic con-
ceptions of God, refusing to identify God as Spirit, if that means
opposed to all that is material, earthly and sexual (aspects with which
women have been identified). Her way of imagining the God of
mystery, unknowable and totally un-capsulatable by human epithets, is
to emphasize the surprising, even shocking dimensions of God, found in
the most unlikely and most despised of places, identified with the most
rejected categories of human beings:

> God will hang on the gallows.
> God will inspire poets and artists.
> God will be battered as a wife, a child, a nigger, a faggot.
> God will judge with righteousness, justice, mercy those who batter,
> burn, sneer, discriminate, or harbor prejudice.
> God will have a mastectomy.
> God will experience the wonder of giving birth.
> God will be handicapped.
> God will run the marathon…
> God will be down and out, suffering, dying.
> God will be bursting free, coming to life, for God will be who God will
> be (Heyward 1984: 26-27).

Re-imagining a God beyond society's limitations and prejudices and
posing radical questions—usually without an answer—form a basis to
her method. But the Bible's central core of justice is also the core of her
theology. As Linda Moody writes: 'For Heyward, God is the source of
justice, resource for justice, maker of justice and justice herself' (Moody
1996: 28).

Clearly *praxis* is at the core of her theology, and the experience of
sexism is the oppression that gives rise to the liberating praxis. Within
this, the injustice of heterosexism, and the discrimination against gay and
lesbian groups is a key focus. Her own stance of coming out as a lesbian

---

4.   See, for example, Owen (1971).

priest, her fierce championing of lesbian rights in Christianity and her courage in enduring the anguish of the ensuing backlash, all show how her theology is embodied in her life at the cost of this particular ministry:

> In the untransformed Christian consciousness, lesbianism is an implicit and bold NO to the God that is limited, by definition, within the categories of light, Logos and Father. The unrepentant lesbian, by her very being—proud and gay—is a sign of new religion/new consciousness/new faith, in which there is no patriarchal authority and no space for male definition of who or what woman is, should be, or will be (Heyward 1984: 39).

But although this struggle is deeply embedded in Heyward's life and is the framework for her work, it does not limit the contours of her work. She has been tireless in uncovering the interconnections with other forms of discrimination: for example, for years she has dialogued with womanist theologians, where racism has formed the core of the discussion; she flew to Nicaragua—with other feminist theologians—in support of the Sandinista regime, and in fact invented the phrase, 'the unfinished symphony of oppression' (referring to the bleak fact that ever more systemic occurrences of injustice continue to raise their ugly heads).

But it is the category of *relationality* which is the most notable feature of Heyward's theology of God, and the category that has influenced many feminist theologians, myself included.[5] This refers to God as the source of right and just relation, because to be God means *to be the source of all just relating*. The sources on which a theology of relation relies are rich. To speak about relating at all, means that this naming of God is rooted and embodied among people, among different types of relationship, among communities of women, men and children. (In my own thinking I extend this to include earth, soil and communities of creatures.) Heyward is inspired by both Martin Buber's *I and Thou* (Buber 1939), and the idea that God created out of a yearning for relation and mutuality. In a beautiful litany inspired by this notion, she wrote,

> And humanity was born in the yearning of God (Heyward 1984: 49).

She was also influenced by the autobiographical works of the Jewish novelist Eli Wiesel, especially where he insists that the Holocaust manifested the power of radical evil as the destruction of and non-existence of power-in-relation:

---

5. See Brock 1988, Keller 1986, Grey 1989, Stuart 1995.

> The Holocaust is experienced as the negation—obliteration, total destruc-
> tion—of relation. To the degree that relation is that which is, for Wiesel,
> radically good, the Holocaust is the experience of radical evil: the extinc-
> tion of the meaning and value of human experience; the nullification of
> human existence; that which is utterly without relation (Heyward 1982:
> 80).

Conversely, the naming of God emerging from within a theology of
relation, is characterized by a thirsting for justice, and is revealed above
all among people who manifest a quality of embodied loving. This
naming is also inclusive of men:

> We are here with God—our Baker woman Mama, our tender Papa, our
> sister-brother-lover God who, when she comes, comes with power!
> (Heyward 1982: 203).

This reveals the second feature of Heyward's theology, namely that God
is revealed through *power*-in-relation or relational *power*: that means in
the actual process of redemption and transformation. And Heyward
believes that divine relational power is successful. God is

> the power that drives to justice and makes it. Makes the sun blaze, the
> rivers roar, the fires rage. And the revolution is won again (Heyward
> 1982: 162).

The power spoken of here, relational power *(dunamis* in the Christian
Scriptures), is contrasted by Heyward with the power of *exousia,* the
institutional power of office. Relational power is passionate, spontaneous,
raw and unpredictable. Heyward depicts it as crucial in the ministry of
Jesus, the embodiment of God's power-in-relation:

> To be in Christ is to share this power of God which drives toward jus-
> tice, the moral act of love between people, black and white, Jew and
> Christian, rich and poor. To be in Christ is to live dangerously...to be in
> Christ is to live with passion...to be with Christ is to realise that God's
> relational *dunamis* is *the* authority under which all authorities—laws,
> Scriptures, traditions, governments, religions and institutions—rise and
> fall (Heyward 1984: 98).[6]

So it is clear that the redeeming power of God, which is so often inter-
twined by feminist theologians with God's creativity (creating and
redeeming as two sides of the same coin), as *the broken web* out of which

---

6.   It may be challenged that Heyward reads back into the New Testament what
are contemporary categories of power. I still argue that the contrast inspires both a
new reading of Scripture and an analytic tool for today's struggle.

the reborn world will emerge,[7] is embodied in the ministry of Jesus, as the earthing in time/space of the Reign of God—and embodied again and again by Christic communities of discipleship.

'Relational power' is part of feminist theology's re-imagining of God's power as alternative to the patriarchal power of the 'God of power and might'. I have tried to see this as the power of sensitivity, of compassion, of empathy, of affiliation and bonding (Grey 1989: 103-104). Catherine Keller muses as to the likelihood of relational power ever winning:

> The lines of relational power, more like fibers in a web than railroad tracks to the horizon, intersect and energise communities of support and struggle already. This latter strategy does not await a Messiah astride his white horse, leading hoards of final angels. Rather, it will nurture the delicate and nonetheless messianic power of awakened relations (Keller 1995: 203).

God as source of power-in-relation, in a further embodying of God[8] within the dynamics of physical relationships, is later linked with the idea *of power as erotic energy* (Heyward 1989). The eros of God, the power which brings healing and wholeness is seen as the 'creating, enlarging and sustaining of relations' (Audre Lorde). It is 'the power which, at its deepest roots, understands joy and refuses injustice' (cited in Grey 1989: 104). Carter Heyward's later theology develops eros as the healing, whole-making power of God (Heyward 1989): but eros has damaging implications for women in different parts of the world.

Lastly, and again within the context of a feminist theological re-envisioning of both transcendence and immanence, Heyward re-images the transcendence of God as the *power of crossing over*, using the imagery of the bridge:

> To transcend means, literally, to cross over. To bridge.
> To make connections. To burst free of particular locations.
> A truly transcendent God knows the bounds of no human life or religion. Such a God is not contained within the holy scriptures or religious creedal formulations.
> No one person, no group of people, has a hot-line to a God who is actually transcendent, for God is too constantly, too actively, moving, crossing over from my life to yours, and from ours to theirs, to become a source of special privilege (Heyward 1984: 245).

---

7.   The reference here is to the title of Keller's book, *From a Broken Web* (1986), and the inspiration is Adrienne Rich's poem, *Integrity* (1980: 9).

8.   The idea of God as *embodied* will be discussed in Chapter 6.

Here is a transcendence cut loose from the remote and controlling traditional imagery, and at the same time linked with the dynamics of redemption; and, interestingly, it still leaves room for immanence as being a many-layered interiority of the dynamic presence of God.

Thus, even though the category of redemptive relationality has been criticized as an inadequate tool to oppose the structures of kyriarchal oppression,[9] it carries the double strength of being rooted in the lived experience of God in relation, a relationality corporately as well as individually understood, as well as issuing from the concreteness of the struggle for justice. The sheer confidence of the metaphor—the assertion that God drives to justice and makes it—can be questioned from the angle of its success in history, but not from the authenticity and depth of its faith and trust in the God of Judaism and Christianity. The breathtaking physicality of some of the language still tends to shock: but did humanity ever understand the implications of God's risk-taking in the mystery of incarnation?

But how does the metaphor work, when springing from the context of the liberation struggles of women from the Two Thirds' World?

God as *Passion for Justice*—Latina and Mujerista Context

'The main principle for our theological work is the Gospel vision of abundant life' writes Maria Pilar Aquino (Aquino 1998: 91):

> Feminist theology adopts an alternative, life-giving logic that promotes the realisation of life in its concrete personal and social dimensions. This logic supports human dignity, the well-being of all, and full participation of all as the central principles for measuring the justice or injustice of society and church (105).

It can be no coincidence that this thirsting for life—in a range of interpretations from sheer survival to a quality of flourishing inclusive of the whole of creation—characterizes the work of women from the Two

---

9.   See Schüssler Fiorenza (1995: 50-57). Keller (1996: 345) comments: 'it is perhaps not surprising that she [Schüssler Fiorenza] has adopted Thistlethwaite's dismissive position on feminist relationalism. So intent is she to equate a liberation hermeneutic with an anti-relationist posture that she identifies leading Asian American theologian Rita Brock's *Journeys by Heart* as a leading perpetrator of main "White lady" theology! Such are the apocalyptic perils of "black-white thinking"' (Reference is to Thistlethwaite 1990: 16).

Thirds' World.[10] It is also no accident that the intercontinental dialogue of women theologians from south and north met around the theme of *Women Resisting Global Violence—A Spirituality for Life*.[11]

It is within this context, as its heart and source, that the mystery of God as *passion for justice* is encountered. But the starting point for Latin American woman theologians is faith, a faith in the God of life. Quite dissimilar from Western and northern contexts, where it is the question of God that is at stake in a secular, 'post-Christian'(?) world, in these contexts it is the question of life itself which is threatened. It is not whether God exists that is in doubt, but how to discover God in a reality of suffering. As Aquino writes in her own book, poignantly titled, *Our Cry for Life*:

> How can we uncover God's true face in a context where women are reduced to insignificance?... What does it mean to speak about the God of life to people whose daily experience is being despised because they are poor women of oppressed races? (Aquino 1993: 131).

Gradually, the images of God as patriarchal lord and judge are being replaced by the image of a God whose special mode of being is one of compassion and mercy. As the link between these traditional images and the oppressed position of women becomes clearer, writes Maria Clara Bingemer, God becomes understood as

> the one who addresses socio-economic and political challenges in the new militancy of Latin American women. The image of God is no longer that of the father to whom one owes submission; rather, God is basically the image of what is most human in woman and man, seeking expression and liberation (Gebara 1989: 44).

Discovering God in the faces of the suffering and oppressed led to the belief that 'faith in God means a commitment to transform this situation' (Aquino 1993: 132). Thus the God of fullness of life becomes the God of the transformation of society.

And this has a specific meaning in the lives of women. As Luz Beatriz Arellano writes:

> being essentially bearers and sustainers of life, women find a new meaning in the discovery of God as God of life; and they themselves become stronger and more conscious as defenders and bearers of life, not only in the biological sense but in all its dimensions (Arellano 1988: 137).

10. Fabella and Oduyoye 1988, Chung 1993, Aquino 1993, Dietrich 1998.
11. See Mananzan, Oduyoye *et al.* 1996.

Thus the meanings of 'fullness of life' found in Latin-American women's experience can in no way be reduced to political utility. Rather, an increased hope in community, in the healed relationship of women and men, an end to *machismo* (the violence characterizing much of women-man relating) and a future for their children—these are the visions of flourishing, the content of faith in the God of life and transformation. As Consuela del Prado writes:

> There are many women in the poor sectors who...go from their own experience of poverty and need to serve the community... Living this way gives them a new sense of the God of Life because it demands that they give up their individualism for the good of the community where they feel they are worth something and their lives and experiences are appreciated. *This is what is meant by living God's call to life in abundance* (del Prado 1989: 142-43, my italics).

But this God of Life is also experienced as a relational God, although in strikingly contrast with the range of life-situations alluded to by Heyward, there is a specific appeal to women's experiences of motherhood. Thus, according to Ana Maria Tepedino, women experience God 'in their own manner, as the One who really protects the weak and is the defender of those who have less life'. She believes, as does Peruvian Consuela del Prado, that since women carry children in their wombs, they experience God differently, in a 'relational' manner, that 'goes beyond conceptual coldness'. Her experience of life embraces 'strength and tenderness, happiness and tears, intuition and reason' (Tepedino and Prado in Moody 1996: 63-64).

This imaging of a relational God as Mother, is based on the biblical image of God's compassionate womb, *rehem,* and developed by Maria Clara Bingemer as a specifically feminine trait of God.[12] The biblical images, she writes,

> allow us to affirm that there exists a feminine principle in the divinity which makes it possible to believe, worship, and love God not only as the strong Father who creates us and liberates us with his powerful arm, but also as a Mother, full of tenderness, grace, beauty and receptivity, who accepts the seed of life and feeds it in her womb, so it may become a full being in the light of day (Bingemer 1989: 67).

12. Clearly, not everyone is happy about what appears a very essentialist division into masculine and feminine, but I present it in fidelity to the diversity of voices. See the discussion in Chapter 2.

Maria Pilar Aquino is aware that not all would agree—specifically, her colleague Elsa Tamez (President of the Biblical Seminary, Costa Rica)— with the use of traditional masculine-feminine archetypes to affirm the motherhood of women, but defends it as important in the new naming of God. Yet she urges caution, as the real problem is the overthrow of the androcentric structures that generated the essentialist archetypes in the first place. According to her, there are other biblical images, as yet unexplored, including Water, Light, Way, Bread, Life, Word, Vine, and Wisdom:

> We are not trying to create an exotic language, but rather to name this ineffable, challenging and loving presence, which became tangible in the strength and vulnerability of Jesus Christ and now acts with life-giving power in the world of the poor and oppressed, in their suffering and their hope, in their weakness and their strength. By naming this presence we are naming ourselves (Aquino 1993: 138).

This imaging of God as relational, life-affirming and present is expressed powerfully by Elsa Tamez in terms of the God of the oppressed, and, specifically including women as both poor and oppressed.[13] But her understanding of oppression goes deeper than political repression: it includes the humiliated bodies of women and men, and the damage to self-esteem, to the inmost dignity of being a person, and includes the lowest level of dehumanization (Tamez 1982: 25). Oppression also includes economic oppression, and this she terms the sin of idolatry, namely, deliberately impoverishing by hoarding economic resources (Tamez in Moody 1996: 61). God's active presence, praxis of justice and availability to all persons are aspects of the way Tamez sees God's embodiment in society. And knowing this God means acting for justice.

That this God of justice is not external to women, but working in and through people of faith, is an aspect of *mujerista* theology, developed especially by Ada María Isasi-Diaz. Although this describes itself as the theology of Hispanic women in the United States, it has many roots and living connections with Latina theology.[14] In the research conducted by

---

13. There are other aspects of Elsa Tamez's theology, for example, her use of pre-Christian sources.

14. As Isasi-Diaz writes (1993: 2-3): 'In addressing whether we should use Latinas or Hispanic women to identify ourselves, the first thing to note is that among ourselves we hardly ever use either of them. Most of us use the national adjective that refers to the countries where we were born, or from where our ancestors came: Cuban, Puerto Rican, Columbian. The only exception to this…are Mexican Ameri-

Isasi-Diaz, even though the actual context is the praxis of justice and liberation, the content of the images of God expressed by the women is that of presence and nearness, and at the same time linked with loyalty to the faith community. When speaking of a woman called Lupe, whom she interviewed, she lets her tell her own story:

> There is the journey to the inside... But I have to reconcile more my two lives, my two worlds as I call them. The world of action as a Christian, what you do, which always has been there, but there is more meaning to that now...and then there is the journey inside, a very personal journey, but that has everything to do with what I do outwardly... God is in me, God is in me. That is why I like myself... I am beginning to understand what I have heard for many years, God speaks more through the poor and in the poor than in anybody else because they do not have anything (Isasi-Diaz 1993: 129).

But this nearness to God, which Lupe has described as connecting the inner and outer experiences, is not necessarily linked with Church. As Lupe says,

> The more I travel into me and come to know God, the more separated I become from my church. It's now to the point that just seeing certain people offends me, just seeing representatives of the institution offends me because they are with power and with money, and they are not with the people (Isasi-Diaz 1993: 132).

What this shows is the linking of deep personal faith and community commitment—in a way that can almost be described as mystical. This leads to a third factor functioning in how God acts for justice. God acts through our passion for just relation, in our commitment to God's passion for justice, and in the depths of God's nearness to us in heart and soul. But God also acts through silence. Elsa Tamez expressed it in these terms:

> without the silence of God we can't become men and women... God remains silent so that men and women may speak, protest, and struggle. God remains silent so that we may become really ourselves. When God is silent and men and women cry, God cries in solidarity with them, but God does not intervene, God waits for the shouts of protest. Then God begins to speak again, but in dialogue with us (Tamez 1985: 175).

cans, who refer to themselves in a way that indicates both their ethnic-national roots and the fact that they are citizens by birth of the USA... Perhaps the difficulty in agreeing on a given word to name the different groups in the USA has to do not only with how disparate we are, but also with the suspicion that by putting us all under one "name" the dominant culture is trying more easily to control and assimilate us.'

This silence of God is sometimes connected with the mystical Dark Night of the soul: in my own work I have described this sense of abandonment as a necessary phase or breakthrough to a new experience of God (Grey 1989, 1997). In this context of God as our passion for just and right relation, I link God's silence with God's compassion and God's suffering with us—two key dimensions arising in feminist theology.

The Compassionate and Suffering God

I am aware that this naming extends wider than the work of feminist theology[15]. But the conviction that 'God weeps with our pain' as the Chinese theologian, Kwok Pui Lan wrote, is a vital part of feminist re-imaging (Kwok 1986). At root, faith in a God who suffers with us does not so much emerge from a philosophical rejection of the impassible, omnipotent and self-sufficient God, but from an experience with a double content: the experience of affliction,[16] of radical suffering which threatens to destroy a sense of being a person, and of the presence of God in this affliction (although not always). But sometimes, the affliction is such that the

> assault reduces the capacity of the sufferer to exercise freedom, to feel affection, to hope, to love God… In radical affliction the soul itself has been so crippled that it can no longer defy evil. The destruction of the human being is so complete that even the shred of dignity that might demand vindication is extinguished (E. Farley 1996: 249).

The anguish surrounding the eruption of this image of God from the suffering of women is bound up with the way so much of this suffering has been hidden, acquiesced in and even exacerbated by the structures of patriarchal society.[17]

15. Since the publication of Jürgen Moltmann's classic, *The Crucified God* (1974), there has been a well-established genre. See Steen (1989) and the bibliography it contains.

16. Simone Weil wrote movingly of experiencing such affliction in her year in the factory (Weil 1950: 122-23), but did not develop the idea in connection with images of God.

17. Think of the way women are given harsher prison sentences for less serious crimes, frequently not allowed to have their babies with them in jail; the scandal of a woman chained to the bed while giving birth (Britain, 1995), encouraged by the then Minister in the Home Office (Anne Widdecombe); the difficulty of getting sentences for rapists; the despising of single mothers, and so on.

The Limits of Human Compassion

This suffering is hardly helped by many people's reaction of powerlessness experienced in the face of overwhelming suffering both at home and at a distance. This 'switching off' from the suffering of others blocks both the extent of their suffering and action to prevent it. 'Compassion fatigue' is a well-known syndrome as we quickly turn off the disturbing TV pictures, or assume that the individuals concerned only have themselves to blame. The psychological and spiritual resources to stay with the painful situation seem to be absent, or deliberately blocked in a consumerist culture, whose interest is continually being focused on the power of spending, a power closely bound up with our culture's definition of personhood as 'I spend, therefore I am'. The resources we do have become channelled to cope with our own personal suffering—the unemployment, illness, housing difficulties of our immediate family and friends: pain is of course sharp and real wherever it occurs.

And yet, even within our frame of experience, there are many groups in society whose resources of caring move far beyond the personal—and this is already a sign of the movement of the human spirit reaching out in empathy beyond mere personal concerns. Nurses and doctors—both male and female—spend the greater part of their day concerned with the pain of others. Social workers (much maligned when things go wrong) focus on the pain of families, distressed and dysfunctional for a variety of reasons.[18] This is without including Charity and Aid workers who are committed to alleviating pain connected with the injustice of structures in a diversity of ways.

So it seems that many human beings are living in a way that continually extends their compassion. The very stress and pressure of life, the emotional demands put on them, does not—except in extreme circumstances[19]—prevent their continuing to care. (People are very creative in discovering stress-alleviating remedies.) Increasingly, there are events and opportunities in life which enlarge the horizons of compassion and engage energies for transforming of injustice. Frequently it is the birth of a disabled child that mobilizes parents' energies to struggle against a par-

18. I am aware that here I beg the question of both the motive for caring, and the scandal of abuse: but the point here is that countless individuals are in fact spending their lives concerned with the pain of others.

19. First among these is the low pay awards for nurses and those in caring professions.

ticular disease. Often it is travel to a country at the time of a catastrophe. In my own case, it was travel to the desert villages and cities of Rajasthan, N. India, as part of my work in the charity 'Wells for India'. Although I saw desperate poverty in the villages—especially among the women—it was the plight of the pavement dwellers of the city that continues to haunt me. Women trying to cook, eat, look after children in filth and squalor. Begging is the only source of income—and sometimes I saw crippled children on all fours crawling in and out of the rush hour traffic trying to beg from cars and rickshaws. How is even the hope for survival kept alive? Memories of the psalms come rushing back—'And you hear the cry of the poor?' But how does God hear the cry of these poor people? They are eking out an existence in the gutters—and who cares if they live or die?

'God weeps with our pain'
But how do we dare to use this suffering as a powerful image of God's own suffering? The conviction comes first of all from the experience of a God who is present and sharing our suffering. Although—as we saw in Chapter 2—the references to God as mother and midwife to the birth of the new Israel are scarce, yet they speak powerfully to the pain of women. The fact that Jesus, about to suffer, compared the pain he would undergo and the subsequent joy, to the travail of women in childbirth (Jn 14) is a sign of the empathy of Jesus, and that this suffering can be creative for the birthing of the Kingdom (or *kin-dom*, as it is frequently called in Christian feminist circles: '*kin-dom*' implies that we are all brothers and sisters in the new creation [Isasi-Diaz 1993: xi]). (Not that the suffering of mothers giving birth in agony and degrading poverty should be idealized.)

Women from a wide diversity of contexts seem to sense that God is not ashamed to share our pain. Indeed, there is an ancient (if minor) tradition that in martyrdom, in witness to the Kingdom, the believer is united with Jesus, the embodiment of God. Christians of the second century saw in the martyred woman Blandina, 'the One who was crucified for them' (Musurillo 1972: 75). The North African slave, Felicitas, about to be thrown to the wild beasts of the arena after just giving birth to her baby, gave witness to Christ redemptively suffering within her (Wilson-Kastner et al. 1981). Contemporary images continue to depict Christ in the form of a woman, in the anguish of giving birth to the new creation.[20]

20. I think especially of Lucy de Souza's painting of 'The Feminine Face of God'

These, one might object, is the suffering love of Christ, not suffering in God's self. But Christian faith trusts that Jesus revealed how God *is*. The passionate love of God for the full humanity of the most marginalized of groups means that God identifies with our pain. But *because God is God, it means that suffering is not all that God does*. God's compassion being poured out ceaselessly is a source of strength for *suffering women*. Knowing that God is with us—even if this God appears powerless in the traditional sense—inspires endurance and courage: the power of compassion is an energy that mutually empowers God and humanity. As Heyward wrote:

> The root meaning of passion or suffering—*passio*—is to bear, to withstand, to hold up. We are called, collectively, to bear up God in the world. To withstand/'stand with' is to be in solidarity with God, to go with God in our comings and goings. This vocation involves pain...but not only pain. To be passionate lovers of human beings, the earth, and other earth creatures; to love passionately the God who is Godself the resource of this love, is to participate in an inspired and mindbogglingly delightful way of moving collectively in history (Heyward 1984: 206).[21]

Wendy Farley, asking what is the character of God's love for us, sees compassion as one of its four characteristics (W. Farley 1990: 97).[22] Within a context of the tragedy of the finite world, the redemptive, healing love of God is ceaselessly active: 'Compassion is divine power in a new guise, the guise of redemption' (111). The power of compassion offers resistance to evil and tragedy and can act as a power of transformation. The compassionate God is God acting redemptively through the power of sensitivity, empathy—encouraging, consoling, remembering us even in the midst of God's own pain and in full realization that the tragic dimension of living will never be overcome. God's very vulnerability[23]

---

that depicts Christ/Christa as Tree of Life, surrounded by the four elements. This picture interweaves aspects of both Hindu and Christian spirituality in a very creative manner.

21. Although it may be pushing the root of '*patio/passio*' as meaning 'suffer, bear' towards the idea of 'bear up', 'hold up', I think it is justified in the sense of the Christian call to take responsibility for the suffering of God.

22. The other three are: ungroundedness, eros and tragedy. I am grateful to Wendy Farley for her analysis of compassion with which I concur—except that I think that God and humanity are more closely caught up with the process of the empowerment of compassion; and that love does not only depend on *separation* for its existence, but on *connection* and that there is always a tension between the two.

23. The issue of theodicy and why God created a world vulnerable to tragedy is

to human suffering and world suffering increases the pain of God.

It is not surprising that images of the God of compassion emerge so strongly in feminist theology, when the lives of poor women in particular are so strongly marked with the struggle to survive, to keep hope alive in the midst of the tragedy of loss, of senseless killing on an immense scale, and with suffering inflicted simply on the grounds of being women.

Holding onto this image of God as hope in the struggle for justice, I now move to explore this in another context.

beyond the scope of this chapter, although the tragic dimension is always present in my mind as I write and will be explored in Chapter 7. See Sands (1994).

Chapter Five

The God who Liberates and who does not Liberate:
The Challenge of Womanist Theology

> If we start from a new premise that God is no longer male and God is not
> made in the image of the dominant culture, women of color can begin to
> reimage ourselves. Women of color can begin to believe that we are also
> created in the image of God. If we, as women of color, are willing to
> reimage and redefine ourselves not as other but as Godlike, then innu-
> merable ways of lifting self-esteem and claiming the right to live whole,
> healthy lives can emerge (Hunter 1993: 191).

As this book progressed I have tried to be faithful to the diversity of new
images of God emerging from feminist theologies all over the world, as
well as to the many connections between these images. I have used the
metaphor of bringing many voices into conversation, into dialogue with
each other and into shared praxis, without blurring differences of economic status, race, culture and sexual preference. So, whereas a certain
similarity is striking in the attempts to move beyond the God the Father
of patriarchy, for example, in imaging God as a God of liberation from
oppression and in privileging words like 'praxis', 'justice', 'embodiment'
and 'mutuality' in the process, the danger is that the distinctiveness of
each context is lost or muted. And nowhere is this more risky than in
womanist theology.

In the first place womanist theology emerged as a powerful movement
among black women in the United States who realized that they had
been betrayed by both black theology and Euro-American feminism.
The male theologians of black theology frequently continued in sexist
attitudes towards the women of their families and overlooked women in
their strategies of liberation. As Toni Morrison described black women's
situation:

Edging into life from the back door. Becoming. Everybody in the world was in a position to give them orders. White women said 'Do this'. White children said 'Give me that'. White men said 'Come here'. Black men said 'Lay down'. The only people they need no take orders from were black children and each other. But they took all of that and recreated it in their own image (Morrison 1970: 109-10).

Black American women, or women of colour, felt very strongly that Euro-American feminism privileged the category of gender, not race, and in so doing overlooked, ignored and therefore continued in their own racism and prejudice:

The pain of oppression is compounded as we experience blatantly racist and other oppressive behaviours from well-intentioned European-American women. These woman want to be known as our sisters, yet they participate in the conspiracy by denying the privilege that is theirs by virtue of the color of their skin. The pain continues when we meet women of color who are unaware that their power and passion have been taken away from them (Hunter 1993: 191).

The word 'womanist' is taken from Alice Walker's *In Search of Our Mothers' Gardens* (1983a), and means 'being womanish', acting grown up, loving other women and working for the survival of the whole people. It also means loving life, music, dance and the Spirit. It is distinguished from feminism as 'purple is from lavender'. Dolores Williams develops this theologically to mean seeing 'poor black folk as the locus of its values' (Moody 1996: 84). Community-building, the quality of life and survival is vital to womanist theology, and this community is extended to mean concern for the whole of human flourishing. For Christian womanist theologians, writes Linda Moody, this means concern for the entire Christian community.

All this is on the basis of suffering as the norm for black women:

For the masses of black people, suffering is the normal state of affairs. Mental anguish, physical abuse and emotional agony are all part of black people's daily lives. Due to the white supremacy and male superiority that pervade this society, blacks and whites, women and men, are forced to live with very different ranges of freedom...the range of freedom has been restricted by those who cannot hear and will not hear voices expressing pleasure and pain, joy and rage as others experience them (Cannon 1989: 282-83).

What white feminism has not understood, it is felt, is what the inheritance of slavery is to the black community, nor the part white women played within it. The narratives of slavery, as Joan Scott put it, are sacred texts for black women (Scott 1997). Nor have white feminist theologians understood the relationship of the history of slavery, the dangerous memory of slavery, to contemporary forms of racism and prejudice in which we are all involved. Recovering the slave narratives of the past as sacred texts means discovering precious sources for survival in the present. This means that the *sources* and *methods* of doing theology are quite distinct.[1]

Sources and Methods

African-American women use a variety of sources in their imaging of the sacred, in particular, the historical memories of slavery and the slave narratives (as has been mentioned), biographies of African-American women, as well as liberation theologies, and the Bible and Church traditions. An extremely rich source for imaging the sacred, and as a source of ethics and moral wisdom, is the creativity of the growing genre of women's literature, as the work of Katie Cannon indicates so well (Cannon 1988).[2] It is impossible to overestimate the importance of these. Locked out of so many structures and privileges of society, black women's literary creativity links with oral narrative traditions, the practices of folk religion, folklore, the consolation and strength of the spirituals and blues traditions, and remembers lost strategies of survival into life:

> The history of these communities, seldom repeated in textbooks, are incorporated into the tales that emphasise the marvelous, sometimes the outrageous, as a means of teaching a lesson. In concert with their African ancestors, these storytellers, both oral and literary, transform gossip, happenings, into composites of factual events, images, fantasies and fables (Christian 1980: 239).

1.   Of course sources and methods of women's theologies and feminist theologies are always diverse. But it is impossible to understand the strength of womanist imaging of God without briefly describing these.

2.   As Cannon writes (1989: 285): 'It is my thesis that the black women's literary tradition is the best available literary repository for understanding the ethical values black women have created and cultivated in their participation in this society... Locked out of the real dynamics of human freedom in America, they implicitly pass on moral formulas for survival that allow them to stand over against the perversion of ethics and morality imposed on them by whites and males who support racial imperialism in a patriarchal white order.'

But in the midst of this rich diversity of sources, this multi-dialogical approach, there is one hermeneutical principle which always stands out: how does the Bible, the tradition of worship and preaching, the literary tradition, affirm and empower the full humanity of black women? And empower black women as mothers and daughters in their whole community? As opposed to the individualism of Euro-America, the womanist tradition is fully community-oriented; whereas much of Western feminism refuses to identify women with motherhood as being an essentializing view of women, 'yet for the womanist, mothering and nurturing are vitally important' (Williams 1989: 183). Indeed, it is a striking feature of womanist novels that the healing of the mother-daughter relationship, so tragically damaged through slavery, is often a strong focus.[3]

It follows from this central principle that womanist imaging of God starts from no abstract, conceptual basis, but from the concrete struggle for survival, for dignity and grace amid the realities of continuing discrimination and oppression. White women's conceptualizing of God is even felt to be a hindrance for the womanist struggle. Womanists do not need to *conceptualize* God as 'our passion for justice', because this is understood as ground and source of their faith. As Jacquelyn Grant writes:

> The source for Black women's understanding of God has been twofold: first, God's revelation directly to them, and secondly, God's revelation as witnessed in the Bible and as read and heard in the context of their experience. The understanding of God as creator, sustainer, comforter and liberator took on life as they agonised over their pain, and celebrated the hope that as God delivered the Israelites, they would be delivered as well (Grant 1989: 211).

But there is an important difference in the way Carter Heyward writes confidently about 'a God who drives to justice and makes it' and the way Dolores Williams understands the story of Hagar (Gen. 16; 21). For example Elsa Tamez had re-interpreted the significance of Hagar as 'the woman who complicated the history of salvation' (Tamez 1986). She specifically recalls the triple oppression of Hagar, so often missed by mainstream interpretation—Hagar suffers as a woman, as Egyptian in a foreign country, and as a slave/concubine. Yet she receives a revelation of God and is the first in the Bible of the mothers of a child foretold. But Dolores Williams sees Hagar's story not as one of liberation, but as one of survival:

3.   I think here of Alice Walker's novel, *Meridian*, and Toni Morrison's *Beloved*.

Hagar's story, insists Williams, was one of human ingenuity for survival. Hagar was not liberated; she merely struggled to beat the odds to survive. Her story of survival is one that has been passed on through the black Church and deserves to be named as a resource for womanist understanding of God (Moody 1996: 90).

The fact that Hagar was not liberated is for Williams crucial for understanding the way African-American women are so frequently hidden and passed over in the categories of many theologies of liberation. This leads her—through a hermeneutic of *identification* and *ascertainment*—to the imaging of a God who both liberates and who does not liberate. A hermeneutic of identification invites theologians to identify the hidden oppressions both in the Bible and in contemporary society. A second movement—ascertainment—asks faith communities to investigate the biases in texts, sermons and songs now being used. With whom have the biblical writers identified or not identified? (Williams 1993: 149, 150).

The Empowering Presence of God

The image of the God who both liberates and does not liberate leads her further to use the motif not of 'black experience' as was used, for example, by James Cone, but of the 'wilderness experience'—hence the title of her book, *Sisters in the Wilderness* (Williams 1993), although the motif is inclusive of women, men and families. This motif also recalls the work of community-building and the struggle for survival of slaves in the desert.

The strand running through womanist imaging of God as the sustainer in the daily struggle of their lives, is further concretized by the encounter with God in Jesus. For Williams, as would follow from her motif of the wilderness, the wilderness is this place of contact: 'If you want to find Jesus, go to the wilderness' (Cannon 1988: 11). Jesus/God/ the Lord are frequently used in a fluid way. Encountering God/Jesus in the wilderness has a transformative effect. Linda Moody notes how this works in different ways: the slave, she writes (1996: 93-94), journeys to the wilderness as a period of isolation away from slavery. Here a relationship is established with Jesus who heals what is in most need of healing. As the slave is converted she is transformed and returns changed in some way.

God is also experienced as a source of sustenance and constant presence (Cannon 1985: 105). Witnessing to the power of Jesus as 'heart fixer and regulator' was a precious memory of Katie Cannon's home life. The power of Jesus—or God in Jesus—gives strength to resist and survive in the midst of suffering. The concept of the embodied God/embodiment of God becomes manifested through human dignity—the dignity of black women insisted on by that great trail-blazer, Zora Neale Hurston.[4] Katie Cannon, in her use of Hurston as a resource, cites her sermons 'Behold de Rib!'[5] and 'The wounds of Jesus' to illustrate the essential equality of all men and women as created in the image of God, 'imago dei'. Another way in which Cannon describes God acting in the lives of black women is through 'quiet grace'—the quality of 'hushed resistance' in their lives:

> Made in God's image, poor Black women move with all the stealth, craftiness, and wisdom of the God Who Knows the Truth in order to effect survival (Moody 1996: 100).

Her third—and linked—notion of God working in the lives of black women is the idea of 'unshouted courage'. This is the

4.   'Zora Neale Hurston (1901?–1960) was the most prolific Black woman writer in the United States. Her mother, Lucy Ann Potts (1865–1904) was a former school teacher and provider of wisdom to Hurston. Though she died when Hurston was only 9 years of age, she left her counsel that her daughter should "jump at de sun... We might not land on the sun, but at least we would get off the ground" ...Hurston's father, John Hurston (1861–1917) was a carpenter and Baptist preacher. In the earliest days of her youth, Hurston heard the rhythmic cadences of Baptist preaching that would later serve as source material in her work to record the folk culture of poor black people in the south' (Moody 1996: 87). A lack of finance meant that by the age of 14 she was living on her own and working as receptionist, wardrobe girl and in many other jobs. Hurston wrote four novels, two books of folklore and an autobiography. She is also famous for rejecting a scholarly anthropological form of writing and attempting to write in the language of 'the folk' with a colourful style and imagination. She is Katie Cannon's chosen resource for womanist theology.
5.   'Behold de rib!
      Brothers, if God
      had taken dat bone out of man's head
      He would have meant for woman to rule, hah
      If he has taken a bone out of his foot,
      He would have meant for us to dominate and rule...
      But, no, God Almighty, he took de bone out of his side
      So dat places de woman beside us;...
      Male and female like God made us.
      Side by side' (Hurston 1990: 141-42). © 1990 HarperCollins Publishers, Inc.

quality of steadfastness, akin to fortitude, in the face of formidable oppression. The communal attitude is far more than 'grin and bear it'. Rather, it involves the ability to 'hold on to life' against major oppositions. It is the incentive to facilitate change, to chip away the oppressive structures, bit by bit, to celebrate and name their experiences in empowering ways (Cannon 1988: 144).

The God of Power and Jesus as Lord

But this God who both liberates and does not liberate is still invoked as a God of omnipotence and power. African-American women differ from their white counterparts in asserting strongly their faith in the omnipotence of God and in Jesus as Lord. Euro-American feminists see addressing Jesus as Lord as a reinforcement of patriarchal, even feudal relations. But for African-American women, calling Jesus 'Lord' is a subversive act. For Jesus is Lord totally differently from the way that the white slave owner was Lord. (Focusing on the life and teaching of Jesus has also been a characteristic of the 'liberal' or 'free' churches for 400 years: focus on Jesus as suffering brother in the struggle is also the core of liberation theologies.)

Similarly, although white feminist theologians have evolved a theology of service in response to New Testament categories, they have—it is felt—left untouched the fact that black women are still locked in humiliating positions of servitude. A study of 1935 tells of the bronx slave market where black women waited to be rented out to white housewives:

> Rain or shine, cold or hot, you will find them there—Negro women, old and young—sometimes bedraggled, sometimes neatly dressed—but with the invariable paper bundle, waiting expectantly for Bronx housewives to buy their strength and energy for an hour, two hours, or even for a day at the munificent rate of fifteen, twenty, twenty-five, or if luck be with them, thirty cents an hour (Baker and Cooke 1935: 330-31).

It is still true that white US middle-class women have educational and professional opportunities because black women are being paid to care for their children and to be responsible for the domestic work. If this is an economic and social problem, it is also a source of pain and alienation between white and black women, meaning that it is premature to talk in terms of sisterhood.

It is also a theological dilemma, writes Jacquelyn Grant (1989: 209): how can it be right to preach a call to a life of service when black women are imprisoned by the most exploitative forms of service? Her answer is to assert that only when Jesus himself has been liberated from white feminist theology can he be reclaimed and discovered for black women. They can then be servants of Jesus, but not in an oppressive sense. Being a servant of Jesus is to be redeemed by him. It is the life, ministry and words of Jesus that are redeeming—for black women his atoning death and suffering are not a focus. Thus the sin of servanthood that black women experience in their lives is overcome by experiencing the call to discipleship.

These are differences indeed and I will not attempt any premature reconciliation between womanist theology and any branch of feminist theology. But it is clear that if the way African-American women relate to God and Jesus is through experiencing in their lives the power of God through the redeeming acts of Jesus, whether this power is experienced as liberating or as power to resist and to survive the suffering and ongoing oppression, that can at least be *compared* with the way other groups of women—both from the north and southern hemispheres—are re-imaging the way divine power works in their lives: not to reinforce the dominant powers of injustice, but to 'raise up the humble' and the marginalized.

A Theology of the Spirit

I have concentrated on the specificity and distinctiveness of womanist theology. But there is one area of exploration that is shared with other groups of feminist theologies and that is the imaging and worshipping of God as Spirit. In other contexts this exploration has partly been inspired by the conviction that God is the Spirit of freedom, transcending both sexes, and refusing identification with a male, patriarchal God. But God as Spirit is not necessarily female even though this identification has been made from time to time.[6]

There are three ways in which God as Spirit is a source of inspiration and rich experience for womanist theologians. The first is in the context of liturgy and worship. As Delores Williams says, the effectiveness of a service is judged, not by the scholarly content of the sermon, ritual, or orderly process, but on the way the power of the Spirit has been experienced (Williams 1989: 185).

6.   See Coakley 1988.

The second way in which the God as Spirit is important is the way in which the Spirit affects and transforms the lives of poor women. Mary's Magnificat is a witness to this—the way that God's Spirit transformed her into becoming Jesus' mother, as God's spirit is lifting up the poorest of women to do God's will. And the third point is the way that the Spirit links with the ancient gods and goddesses who empowered poor people to resist injustice before the coming of Christianity. Here, womanist theologians explore the relationship between the Holy Spirit of Christianity and the spirit(s) of African-based traditions.[7] This is becoming a very rich area, encouraged by the Alice Walker's definition of womanists as those *who love the spirit*. In *The Colour Purple*, the Spirit is described by Shug to Celie as

> God is inside of you and inside everybody else. You come into the world with God. But only them that search for it inside find it out. And some-time it just manifest itself even when you not looking, or don't know what you looking for (1983: 177).

Whereas there is some tension as to whether Alice Walker's idea of spirit is necessarily a *Christian* one (and, if not, should the term womanist apply to *Christian* theologians?), Emilie Townes has suggested that Alice Walker's idea of the immanent God can be compared with the African-American 'walking with Jesus' and she wants to uphold Walker's con-cept of the sacred as 'woven intricately into the very fabric of existence itself' (Townes 1989: 95).

What this study wants to build on is the way that 'the Spirit' functions across a range of women-centred theologies, keeping alive the spark of hope, the memories of a strong cultural past to transform the present, and nurturing solidarity and community. It was the power of this spirit that Toni Morrison was describing in her monumental novel *Beloved*, where Baby Suggs, that great-spirited leader, summoned the people— almost broken by struggles against slavery— into the forest:

> Then she shouted, 'Let the children come!' and they ran from the trees towards her.
> 'Let your mothers hear you laugh,' she told them, and the woods rang. The adults looked on and they could not help smiling.
> Then 'Let the grown men come,' she shouted. They stepped out one by one from the ringing trees.

7.   I realise that Goddess traditions have already been discussed: here the specifi-city of the Holy Spirit connecting with the spirit(s) of other faiths and of pre-Christian traditions is the issue.

'Let your wives and your children see you dance,' she told them, and the groundlife shuddered under their feet.

Finally she called the women to her. 'Cry', she told them. 'For the living and the dead. Just cry.' And without covering their eyes the women let loose (Morrison 1987: 87-88).

Here is divine power in action through the strong leadership of a woman, the divine power of the Spirit, and a sustaining and nurturing community.

These examples of the sacred in African-American literature open up a new way of imagining the sacred, here in the context of resistance to violence and injustice. It is a trail followed also in other contexts, especially by some African and Asian women theologians. And it is to the complexity of the cultural issues raised in these contexts that I now turn.

Chapter Six

An Embodied God

'Here,' she said, 'in this place here, we flesh; flesh that weeps, laughs; flesh that dances on bare feet in grass. Love it. Love it hard. Yonder they do not love your flesh. They despise it. They don't love your eyes; they'd just as soon pick em out. No more do they love the skin on your back. Yonder they flay it. And O my people they do not love your hands. They only use, tie, bind, chop off and leave empty. Love your hands! Love them. Raise them up and kiss them. Touch others with them, pat them together, stroke them on your face 'cause they don't love that either. *You* got to love it, *you*!' (Morrison 1987: 88).

There can hardly be a more moving passage in contemporary literature where the need to love bodies which have been abused and violated is described as an urgent priority for healing. Here the bodies are those of women, men and children and the context is the slavery of the black community in the United States. Baby Suggs, a woman of great authority, leads her people to healing by teaching them to love their own despised bodies.

In the context of colonial Korea, the theologian Chung Hyun Kyung tells the story of Soo Bock, captured by Japanese soldiers and forced to become a so-called 'comfort woman':

> Starting in the afternoon and through the night they [= Korean women] had to receive the Japanese soldiers. Sometimes they received more than sixty soldiers a day. If they resisted, they were stripped and whipped in front of Japanese soldiers in the military field... Many women started to die of starvation, exhaustion, and venereal diseases, and from their wounds from being battered by Japanese soldiers (Chung 1996: 131).

But the extraordinary point about Soo Bock was that, unlike the other women, she decided to survive and began to eat. Again, respecting bodily needs was the beginning of not only healing but sheer survival.

These examples can be multiplied the world over: but what have they to do with our understanding of God? In previous Chapters I have described the way in which women have experienced God within their own bodies—'I found God within myself and I loved her, I loved her fiercely' (Shange 1976). In Chapter 2, 'Encountering God as "She"' I stressed that we cannot underestimate the healing value of rituals focusing on reverencing female bodies where these have been despised throughout the religious traditions. Then, in Chapter 4, 'God—our Passion for Justice' I explored the faith in a God 'who Weeps with Our Pain' (Kwok 1986), suggesting that experiencing a God who identifies with the violated bodies of women has given many women hope of healing and redemption.[1] In a tradition where, as Carol Christ has written, 'She may see herself like God only by denying her sexual identity' (Johnson 1994: 38), the experience of having female sexuality affirmed can be overwhelming.

But we touch here on the chief paradox of classical theology. On the one hand, we are taught that the word 'God' is not so much referring to a person but to the whole *mystery of being*—hiddenness, ultimacy and incomprehensibility being hallmarks of this; and that we may only refer to God by analogy, and by analogies that have been well tested and approved by tradition—but on the other hand we are confronted by a God whose chosen means of revelation is through incarnation, flesh-taking, in other words through being embodied in creation. I argue in this chapter that insufficient weight is given to the scandalous implications of the embodiment of God; that we cheapen this amazing metaphor by narrow arguments as to whether God can be embodied as male or female, and by reducing God's embodiment solely and exclusively to incarnation in Jesus Christ; and that by allowing ourselves to be grasped by some of the deeper meanings of this metaphor, we both enrich our understanding of God and cannot escape confronting the areas of ambiguity and tragedy I have alluded to earlier.

Resisting the Embodying God

The first point is that resistance to the embodying God stems from the fear that this is reductionist, even blasphemous. How can the Almighty,

---

1. This, of course, has been one of the consequences of the Christa figure—that Christ as a woman on the Cross has been experienced by many abused women as identifying with them and hence as a saviour for them.

Transcendent God be embodied in female, violated flesh? For some, this is a shocking suggestion. In this context, it is clear that theologians in the early Church found great difficulty in explaining Mary's childbirth in giving birth to Jesus of Nazareth, except in de-physicalized terms. Not only was the conception of Jesus understood as having nothing to do with a sexual act, but this childbirth was seen as miraculous and pain-free, and the breast-feeding of Jesus by Mary given scant theological attention. Mercifully, this was not neglected by mediaeval art that depicts the tenderness and intimacy of the maternal relation,[2] or by the Eastern Orthodox icon tradition, which honours Mary as Theotokos, God-bearer.

But let us agree for the moment that there is no sub-plot being suggested here for reducing the mystery of God. Let us suppose that Elizabeth Johnson is right in suggesting that 'a renewal of the discovery of God for our age may well begin by a deepened experience of God's inconceivability' (Johnson 1994: 111). Indeed, it is the limitations of technology, the misery felt by the failure of material goods to produce happiness that has fuelled anew the quest for God in our times. Poll after poll informs us that even if people are leaving the Churches, they do not give up on the belief in the mystery of life. The sheer popularity of spirituality courses, retreats and spiritual direction witnesses to this search.

How, then, can the contradiction between 'mystery', 'the hidden God' and the scandalous particularity of the God revealed as embodied, be understood?

The first clue is given by the nature of metaphorical and analogical language itself. Our entire lives are interwoven with metaphorical language (Soskice 1985, McFague 1982). The very processes of our being and becoming occupy the space—or operate in the tension—between body/spirit, fact/interpretation, receptivity/activity and rationality/emotion. A slice of bread is never merely so many ounces of flour—except in the recipe for making it—but what sustains us for the morning, what gives us hope (the bread of life, bread in the wilderness, bread as wisdom), or, as 'the last crust', what tests our abilities to share. As human persons in relationship, someone can be 'a source of joy', 'the bane of my life', 'the poison or passion of my existence', or the 'light of my life'.

---

2.   Yet, Janet Wootton, in her book in this series (Wootton 2000), points out that Christian Rossetti's Christmas Hymn, 'In the Bleak Midwinter', has a final verse referring to Mary's feeding of Jesus, 'A breastful of milk, and a manger full of hay'— but that this verse is frequently omitted.

Not only that, but events, moments and places are sites of metaphoric meaning. 'Jerusalem the Golden with milk and honey blest' is a condensed metaphor, a combination of many images. At the beginning of the third millennium we are building on a condensed nucleus of utopian images, so that we do not merely refer to a point in time, but to a significant point, swinging on a fulcrum between Armageddon and the New Jerusalem—and political discourse makes great play of this ambiguity.

So, similarly, to refer to God in metaphoric terms, as the Scriptures and tradition have consistently done, should not intrinsically encourage us to lose touch with rootedness in our bodily contexts. The problem is the inheritance of a body-denying tradition and the low opinion of women's bodies in particular.[3] If we are convinced that even in the most intimate relationship we do not possess the being of the other, yet we do experience the physicality of the other, why should we fear to use embodied imagery for God, if we likewise—or even more so—keep ourselves aware that metaphors do not grasp but interpret experience, and that each metaphor is limited? And if, in the true tradition of Aquinas, we realize that if our metaphors in describing our own relationships fall short, how much more will they do so in the case of God? It is therefore to say with Paul, yes, 'we do see through a glass darkly', but *we do see*, and we take on trust that what we see is not contradicted by the hiddenness and the mystery we cannot see. Even more, *the glass is not broken*, and we can trust what is revealed. So, when, in the following passage, Thomas Merton writes of the vulnerability of God as seen in the homeless man/woman, we have to take this vulnerability seriously and ask how this is to be understood if we also believe in the power and transcendence of God. As he writes so poetically:

> The shadows fall. The stars appear, the birds begin to sleep. Night embraces the silent half of the earth. A vagrant, a destitute wanderer with dusty feet, finds his [her] way down a new road. A homeless God, lost in the night, without papers, without identification, without even a number, a frail expendable exile lies down in desolation under the sweet stars of the world and entrusts Herself to sleep (Grey, Heaton and Sullivan 1994: 171).[4]

What has happened previously is not only that we have not taken sufficient care over our language for the divine, to see if the metaphors

3.   See, in this series, *Introducing Body Theology* (Isherwood and Stuart 1998).
4.   Merton did write 'his' and referred to God as 'Himself'. I have taken the liberty of changing the pronoun.

are still alive and vibrant and convey what they are intended to convey—for example, the Lord/serf metaphor belongs to the feudal system, and not to the attempts to build democracy, yet the language remains, and frequently serves to cover up unjust relationships, as do military and judicial metaphors; but also, by insisting on the canonical and historical veracity and privileged status of such metaphors, we have prevented the revelatory power of others from evoking a richer spiritual experience.

What I now explore is this richer promise of the metaphor of an embodied God. Whereas feminist liberation theology will never relinquish the vital link between this metaphor for God and the healing of violated women—and all vulnerable people—the urgency of this leads us into a still wider significance for God's embodiment in the whole of creation to be discovered, and embodiment as a metaphor for the activity and agency of God in the world.

The World as the Body of God

This metaphor has been explored most recently by Sallie McFague (1987, 1993, 1997), a feminist and eco-theologian.[5] Her exploration has the aim of transforming our sensibilities about the urgency of the environmental crisis and awakening the human community to take proper responsibility—a reaction that will demand far more energy and commitment than a certain amount of recycling and the occasional use of public transport. If the world was seen through the metaphor of God's Body, she argues, could we recover the sense of the world as sacred, lose our arrogance as 'kings of creation' and start to occupy our proper space, instead of ruining the space for all living things? This is the challenge of the metaphor.

What gives confidence is that the word 'body' has a world of metaphoric meanings in the English language, from civic corporations to 'a body of work', so that there is no way that the world as 'the Body of God' can be thought of as a mere literal description.[6] Again and again it is repeated that there can be no descriptions of God, but 'everything can be a metaphor for God' (McFague 1993: 134).

But, whereas 'The Body of God' is not identical with bodies of women, men or living creatures, what gives the metaphor force within

---

5.   Although a trail was blazed earlier by Grace Jantzen, *God's World, God's Body* (1984).

6.   There will be other worlds of metaphoric meanings evoked in other languages.

the Christian tradition is that the Body has a Christic shape. This means that God's body identifies—just as Jesus did—with the bodies of the poor, suffering and oppressed. So, because women's bodies have traditionally been a site of conflict, 'where we see both worship and loathing of bodies' (24), to consider women's bodies (and not only the bodies of women) as '*the Body of God*' could bring enormous hope in the situations of slavery and brutality with which this chapter began.

What is more, the metaphor encourages us to see the earth as our true home, and not to locate it out in space, in a disembodied heaven, as many a traditional hymn expresses it:

> Man is lonely by birth,
> Man is only a pilgrim on earth;
> Born to be King,
> Time is but a temporary thing,
> Only on loan while on earth (Miriam Thérèse Winter).[7]

In loving the earth, in recognizing our rightful place among all living organisms (sin, in this theory, means the refusal to accept our rightful place), a new way of understanding the transcendence and immanence of God is revealed:

> It is not a model of transcendence in which God is King and the world is the realm of a distant, external ruler who has all power and expects unquestioned obedience from his subjects, human beings. Nor is it a model of immanence in which God the King once entered the world by becoming a servant in the form of one human being. Rather, it is a radicalisation of both divine transcendence and immanence. The model of the universe as God's Body radicalises transcendence for *all* of the entire fifteen-billion-year history and the billions of galaxies is the creation, the outward being, of the One who is the source and breath of all existence (McFague 1993: 133).

In this enlarged view of transcendence, the important fact implied here is that God's transcendence is not available *except* as embodied. Immanence is likewise radicalized, and is seen as a presence paradigmatically in Jesus of Nazareth but also in and through all bodies, 'the bodies of the sun and moon, trees and rivers, animals and people' (McFague 1993: 133). This re-imaging of transcendence and immanence is a notable feature of feminist imaging of the divine. What links many of these explorations is a determination to see the tension not as a polarity, but as

---

7.   Every effort has been made to trace the copyright owner without success. Anyone claiming copyright should contact Sheffield Academic Press.

a mutually enriching contrast, and one that is not given crude gender application. In Chapter 4 in the context of the passion for right and just relation, I quoted Carter Heyward's re-imaging of transcendence as 'the power of crossing over' and immanence as a many-levelled interiority.

The thrust of many feminist and ecological attempts is to depict the cosmic and creative power of God in the widest possible way—linking with expressions in science, art, poetry and music—without losing the rootedness of God's power in creation and not to understand divine power exercised as something extrinsic to it. This is still not to limit God's transcendent power to our own world nor to reduce its mystery to its observable operations.

At the other point of tension God's immanent presence is experienced even in the lowliest member of creation—an experience that Julian of Norwich witnessed to with a hazel-nut, and many mystics similarly. Feminist liberation theologians will always ground divine immanent presence in a privileged manner in suffering bodies, and witness to the experience God even in chaos, mess, disorder and disruption. They raised questions, too, about the bodily experience of God as sexual and erotic experience.

Erotic Experience as Experience of God

> The divine is always becoming flesh—what else does eros desire? Of course, stories of God becoming Man have eclipsed the revelation of Her becoming woman. But now, in our becoming, visions begin slowly to clear (Keller 1986: 250).

This is a highly provocative area and one which can seem both shocking and self-indulgent to many, lacking any roots in Christian tradition. It is explored mainly by Carter Heyward, and seems a natural progression from her earlier work on God as power-in-relation (discussed in Chapter 4). It is Heyward who makes the specific connection between God and erotic power seen as sacred power. Erotic power is simply the felt sensuous connection between ourselves, animals and the living earth experienced as *good* energy. Heyward says more:

> The erotic is our most fully embodied experience of the love of God. As such, it is our capacity for transcendence, the 'crossing over' among ourselves, making connections between ourselves in relation. The erotic is the divine spirit's yearning, through our body selves, towards mutually empowering relation, which is our most fully embodied experience of God as love (1 Jn 4.7ff) (Heyward 1989: 99).

This is clearly a widened meaning of erotic, far from the degraded connotations of contemporary society. It is akin to Matthew Fox's re-imaging of the eros as part of his creation spirituality (Fox 1981, 1983). Eros according to the latter is *making the most of your natural ecstasies,* such as running barefoot in a pine forest, and re-awakening to joyful connections with nature. Matthew Fox, like Heyward, praises the goodness of bodily feeling in the face of a history of its being denigrated in favour of soul, mind and spirit. Both do so aware of the split between eros and agape, where eros is seen as self-centred, an orientation to be renounced in favour of agape, or other-centred love—even if there are now attempts to overcome this damaging split.[8] But Heyward does so more daringly, in that she crosses the line between *acceptable* bodily delight and what is termed by French feminism *the abject* (Kristeva 1982).[9] The abject refers to what is polluted and taboo in many societies.[10] Insofar as the female body has been treated as polluted, shameful, and surrounded with taboos and rituals of exclusion, it has been an *object of abjection.* Reclaiming eros is thus at the same time reclaiming the goodness of *female* bodily experiences.

Heyward then argues that recovering eros as source of relational power is to deepen our experience of the divine:

> We begin to realise that God moves among us, transcending our particularities. She is born and embodied in our midst. She is ground and figure, power and person, this creative spirit, root of our common life, and of our most intensely personal longings. As the wind blows across the ocean, stirring up the sea creatures, causing them to tumble, rearranging them, the erotic crosses over among us, moving us to change the ways we are living in relation (Heyward 1989: 102).

As with the previous insight of God as power-in-relation, this re-imaging of eros as the yearning of God as the core of embodied life is inspirational. Another area of mutuality is created that can be seen as part of the recovery of the goodness of sexual feeling: erotic power as

8. See, for example, Avis (1989).

9. Heyward does not use this term and, as far as I know, has not engaged with French feminism.

10. 'Abjection appears as a rite of defilement and pollution in the paganism that accompanies societies with a dominant or surviving matrilineal character. It takes the form of the exclusion of a substance (nutritive or lined with sexuality), the execution of which coincides with the sacred since it sets it up' (Kristeva 1982: 17).

holy. As holy it stands in direct opposition and rejection of distorted forms such as sadomasochism and pornography. They are to be opposed as *wrong relation*. But re-instating eros may only be able to have limited use, as it seems not to give sufficient weight to the grim reality that thousands of women and young girls are forced to live out degraded and violent forms of eros, as victims of a system they are powerless to change. Although Heyward never separates love and justice, it seems to me that reclaiming eros, re-imaging God as source of erotic power, is not the most helpful category for these contexts. Even where the situation is not one of prostitution but of marriage, in many parts of the world this experience is one of life-long poverty and drudgery, where to speak of eros almost seems a mockery. Survival, solidarity and sustaining hope are rather the specific dimensions of divine sacred power where bodies of women are so systemically misused.

But the discussion does raise the question, first, as to whether it is possible to say where God is not, and again, the possibility of harmonizing the presence of the Body of God with ambiguity and tragedy.[11] Further, if the earth is the Body of God, being welcomed, sheltered and given a home by the Body of God is a way of experiencing the hospitality, the home-making of God. Again this is a way of developing the metaphor from a simplistic identification with either the body of a man or woman towards understanding the hospitable earth with all her generosity, and the way the giving and receiving of hospitality forms the core of Christian lifestyle, all as an integral part of the Body of God.

The Hospitality of God[12]

This metaphor is at the heart of the biblical tradition and ancient Near Eastern spirituality. That the famous Russian icon painter, André Roublev—(and of course, the iconic tradition before him)—could take the scene from Gen. 18.1-8, where Abraham entertains the three angelic messengers to a meal, believed by the Russian Orthodox icon tradition to be a symbolic representation of the Holy Trinity, speaks volumes for the hospitality of God and the centrality of the Eucharistic meal. We now know that when Jesus cites the fate of Sodom (Lk. 10.12), on the

---

11. See the following Chapter.

12. This metaphor has been explored as an ecclesial metaphor in the theology of Letty Russell, *Church in the Round* (1993).

occasion of sending out the 72 disciples, it is in the context of violated hospitality and nothing to do with homosexuality.[13]

For women, the whole area of hospitality is ambiguous. The beginning of this chapter told the painful story of one of the so-called Korean 'comfort women'. But this story can be endlessly repeated in different contexts throughout Asia—and not only Asia. As Aruna Gnanadason has written:

> In Asia the structural violence against women and such patriarchal institutions, such as family, marriage, Christian personal laws, sexist liturgical practices, and low participation of women in the church and its ministry and in the society, have not yet been analysed theologically, nor have they been recognised as 'sins' against half the people of God (Gnanadason 1988: 73).

Thus, structural violence against women—rape, dowry deaths, female infanticide, prostitution encouraged by a mafia of politicians, businessmen and police—is the systemic sin of violence. Pornography in its truest sense is *not eros (or even sex) but violence.* As we have seen, it causes difficulties in imagining eros at the heart of God. As experienced in debased forms, it seems rather a violation of the Body of God. Further, this form of 'hospitality' which women are being forced to give men degrades their whole being and robs them of basic human dignity. Yet literary representations of prostitution can even be idealized—as, for example, the figure of Sonia in Dostoevsky's *Crime and Punishment.*[14]

Mostly, hospitality in our homes rests on the labour of women. In many countries—even if in the West this is slowly changing—it is still true that the women who prepare the meals do not eat with the guests—as it would have been in the time of Jesus and the New Testament Churches. Yet hospitality—welcoming the stranger—was indisputably built into the Jewish culture. It remains a high value still in many eastern countries, where, as I have experienced in India, 'the guest is next to God'. There is still a deep awareness—as there was in Celtic Christianity and the Orthodox Liturgy—that the gifts of the earth—crops, water, trees and the warmth of the sun, are all part of God's generosity. It is this bountiful hospitality that sustains life. And evokes constant thanksgiving.[15]

---

13. In any case, the Genesis passage refers to the proposed rape of the three visitors by the men of the town and not to the question of the goodness of same-sex relations.

14. See my discussion of this point in Grey (1993: 30-32).

15. See the text of the old Celtic rune which expressed hospitality so beautifully in Grey and Zipfel (1993).

Hospitality forms an integral part of the spirituality of African women, even if materialist values infiltrating urban life now threaten it.[16] Mercy Amba Oduyoye, citing the sociologist Felicia I. Ekejuiba, proposes the term 'hearthhold' (not household) to express the reality that African families are centred around the hearths of women (Oduyoye 2001). This, writes Oduyoye,

> agrees with the images of God as Mother in some traditions and as provider and sustainer in Christianity. It agrees also with images of the compassionate Jesus who cared so much for the physical and mental well-being of all he encountered; it also fits with the Holy Spirit, the advocate and comforter, many of whose attributes reflect the mothering that African society depends on (Oduyoye 2001).

Within an understanding of the entire creation as the hearthhold of God (and this image becomes central to Oduyoye's theology of Church), the hearthhold of Christ occupies a space within this in a non-triumphalist manner, that does not deny hospitality to other hearthholds (other religions).

So, because hospitality is rooted in God, it is a cornerstone of African women's spirituality. Because of the ambiguity regarding women's bodies already referred to, African women are sensitive to the kinds of hospitality that make them less than human. Respect for women's bodies is honouring the hospitality of God. Not only women's bodies but the entire natural world demands care, respect and honour. Not only is this a demand of justice and compassion, but follows from our 'being created in the image' of God. So a reconceptualization of hospitality is required. This, says Oduyoye, 'must begin with women learning to be hospitable to themselves, 'to not allow the invasion of their bodies, gifts from God, temple of God and inescapable part of our humanity'.

But honouring the body as part of God's hospitality does not mean eclipsing the Spirit. Rather, as I explore the way through the metaphor of the world as the body of God, we can understand the activity of the Spirit in a deeper way, yet one that has always been integral to the Jewish and Christian traditions.

16. Oduyoye's book develops this point at some length, pointing out that degrading poverty is forcing men back to the villages, seeking an infantile form of mothering, and thus a less appropriate form of hospitality.

The Holy Spirit—Breath of the Body

If the world is understood as the Body of God, the hospitable Father/ Mother of creation, and if the shape of the Body is Christic, the Church being the hearthhold of Christ (for the Christian tradition), then the creative Spirit is the life-giving and sustaining breath of the Body. There is an enormous weight of tradition given to the creative role of the Spirit, the holy *Ruach,* active at the dawn of creation, the wind of God sweeping over the deeps (Gen. 1.1).[17] As the prophetic spirit, God has energized the prophets and the prophetic mission of Jesus (Lk. 4.18-30). But, through the over-spiritualized, body-denying tradition, we have lost the embodying of the Spirit in creation, in the earth, the sense that energy is material energy, incarnate in human bodies, animal bodies, all living organisms and cosmic dust.

We catch a glimpse of this energizing God, in the biblical imagery of God as eagle, captured poetically by the hymn—'and I will raise you up on eagles's wings'; but even the traditional imaging of the Spirit as a dove has been tamed and trivialized. A student of mine, years ago, confronted with giving a class on the Holy Spirit, came seeking help, without much idea as to the theology involved. I showed her some famous mediaeval pictures and light dawned. 'Why, *he*'s only the pigeon!' she said with some relief. As Spirit, God is the life-principle and breath of every organism (the immanent God). But as Spirit, God is also the energy empowering the growth of the entire universe (the transcendent God). Nor should we create unnecessary oppositions between prophetic and creative Spirit on the one hand, and the mystical Spirit on the other—so powerfully expressed in the Romantic poets. Gerard Manley Hopkins wrote about the renewing force of the Spirit in a well-loved poem:

> There lives the dearest freshness deep down things,
> And though the last lights off the black West went
> Oh, morning at the brown brink eastward, springs—
> Because the Holy Ghost over the bent
> World broods with warm breast and with ah! bright wings ('God's Grandeur'
> in Hopkins 1953: 27).

Here he managed in one fell swoop to capture creativity, tenderness, redeeming power, mystical presence and animal warmth. It would seem

17. See, for example, the already-mentioned book of John Taylor (1972).

that the special aspect of the Spirit's activity—in the context of the metaphor we are exploring—is a *connecting* function:

> The connection is one of relationship at the deepest possible level, the level of life, rather than control at the level of ordering and directing nature… Thus, in a spirit theology, we might see ourselves as united with all other living creatures through the breath that moves through all parts of the body, rather than as demilords who order and control nature (McFague 1993: 145).

The connecting function—Taylor had already described the Spirit as the *Go-between God* (1972)—is not merely a rational function of understanding ecological connections; nor is it chiefly didactic in the sense of humbling us to realize our rightful part of creation, important as this is; it is as an energizing function, the discovery of the vitality at the heart of the universe, once we choose to participate in 'the dance of creation' that the power of the Spirit is continually revealed. And this vitality energizes body, mind and heart with an integrating energy. (Integrating energy is how I understand the unitive function of the Spirit.) Grace works through integration not separation. The Spirit is the binding energy expressed by the word *re-ligio/religion*—a word that itself reflects the brokenness and fragmentation of the universe, that God is trying to heal.

And this is why we can speak of the grief of the Spirit (Eph. 25.30).[18] This is the pain of the Body of God at the extinction of a bird or animal, or the ravaging of the rain forest. That part of the world, seen as the Body of God, is dead, or rather killed by another part of the Body. Yet, the Spirit though seeking embodiment in history, is ever free, refuses to be limited by identification in one body or another and resists any premature foreclosure. And as the Spirit of Wisdom, *hokmah, sophia,* this relation of all relations bursts through the chains in which we try to shackle her, showing us time and time again, *that God will be God…*

It is in the search for Spirit-Sophia that many lines of exploration begin to converge—only to branch out again, as the spiralling dance whirls on. Yet, keeping close to the physicality of the metaphor of the body, it is not the transcending-into-space dimension of the Spirit that is

---

18. 'And do not grieve the Holy Spirit of God…' (Eph. 4.30).

here the focus, but warmth and nearness, God as 'a warm, moist, salty God' (Edwina Gateley):

> Deep in myself
> I found my God
> stirring in my guts,
> my middle-aged bones,
> stilling all my buts.
> There where my spirit
> had slumbered long,
> numbed into a trance,
> A moist, warm, salty God
> arose,
> and beckoned me to Dance (Gateley 1993: 90).[19]

19. Edwina Gateley © 1993 Source Books, Trabuco Canyon, California. Reproduced from *A Warm Moist Salty God*.

Chapter Seven

Tragedy in God

For all the pain you suffered, my mama. For all the torment of your past and future years, my mama. For all the anguish this picture of pain will cause you. For the unspeakable mystery that brings good fathers and sons into the world and lets a mother watch them tear at each others' throats. For the Master of the Universe, whose suffering world I do not comprehend. For dreams of horror, for nights of waiting, for memories of death...for all these I created this painting—an observant Jew working on a crucifix, because there was no aesthetic mould in his own religious tradition into which he could pour a painting of ultimate anguish and torment (Potok 1972: 329).

The poignant story of the young artist, Asher Lev brings us into the area of what place tragedy has in God. Classical theology has found it very difficult to accept ambiguity and tragedy in God, as I have hinted throughout this book—for example, in the challenge of the Jewish feminist theologian, Judith Plaskow (Chapter 3). Yet, as tragedy is indisputably a dimension of life on this planet and, because it is one expression of the embodiment of God, it must somehow find its rootedness in the nature and mystery of God. Yet, in theology, we find it either ignored, or trivialized on the one hand, or robbed of meaning because we rush to give it premature resolution on the other.

The tragic dimension poses the question that never goes away, as to whether there is any positive meaning to existence at all; it is a dimension that has become fashionable in this *fin de siècle* mood to identify with a kind of terminal pessimism, the death of hope, the collapse into apocalypticism. Yet feminist liberation theology finds itself confronted at every point by tragic suffering that appears to have no resolution: to ignore it, or to repeat this premature resolution would be to betray the very communities constitutive of our identity.

First, I argue that what is commonly called *the tragic* is actually a narrowing of the whole dimension of tragedy. Secondly, I will show that traditional answers to the challenge posed by the tragic dimension actually prevent deeper exploration into the nature and agency of God. I then present and critique two widely differing approaches to tragedy from feminist theologians: while I have certain disagreements with them both, I suggest that they have succeeded in moving us out of the impasse of classical theology and opened up new directions, thus enabling new approaches to sources of Christian faith.

Tragedy or Tragic Posture?

A gigantic tidal wave wipes out entire villages in Papua New Guinea: thousands are drowned and thousands are homeless. In the Sudan it seems like a whole civilization agonizes its way to starvation. In Turkey, an earthquake kills thousands, and many more are homeless. In Europe and North America increasing numbers of people eke out ten or even twenty years in the lingering, humiliating death of Alzheimer's disease. In a village I know in the desert of Rajasthan an old man sat in tears knowing his life was a failure—he had failed to provide water for his children and grandchildren. Life was not sustainable. The catalogue goes on: these are but a few images—anyone might have selected a variety of experiences to count as tragic. Tragedy, it would seem, is with us not only as a dimension which, like death, threatens with the limits of mortality and personal finitude; but also as threatening the very possibility of making rational sense of planetary life at all.

The twentieth century was a time when the question was increasingly raised, post-holocaust, post-Hiroshima, not only 'Where is God?', but 'Can there be God?' What kind of deity could permit these tragedies, apart from a tragic God or even an evil God?

But is it right to start here? To start with the idea that tragedy is synonymous with catastrophe? The theologian Louis Ruprecht objects:

> Today, everything is a tragedy—planes hijacked by terrorists, children trapped in a lunatic cross-fire, earthquakes, famines, floods—catastrophe in any form. Tragedy seems to connote catastrophe, pure and simple, but in the process of telling ourselves this many times we have trivialised, through overuse, a word that was anything but trivial (Ruprecht 1994: 90).

Ruprecht's study argues that what we are loosely calling tragic, namely, all kinds of catastrophes, is actually a narrowing of tragedy to *tragic posture*. It is indisputable, he writes, that tragedy involves suffering, but

> while we all suffer, not all suffering is tragic… It is what I am equipped to do with my suffering, the Destiny that I carve out of my Fate, that defines and alone is capable of defining the tragic (Ruprecht 1994: 91).

I suspect that what Ruprecht calls 'the tragic posture'—the kind of gloom and doom thinking, the apocalyptic mindset, which attends what I call 'the decline and fall of the second millennium' (Grey 1998) is close to what the American feminist theologian Sharon Welch called the 'cultured despair of the middle-classes' (Welch 1990: 14-47):

> The temptation to cynicism and despair when problems are seen as intransigent is a temptation that takes a particular form for the middle-class. This does not mean that those who are poor or working class are not damaged by or susceptible to despair… But the despair of the affluent, the despair of the middle-class has a particular tone: it is a despair cushioned by privilege and grounded in privilege… When the good life is present or within reach, it is tempting to despair of its ever being in reach for others and resort merely to enjoying it for oneself and for one's family (15).

Both these descriptions imply there can be a kind of hypocrisy in the too-speedy invoking of the tragic dimension, the facile re-naming of our age as the new Dark Ages, as Alasdair McIntyre did at the end of *After Virtue* (1981).

Despite this, another problem is that post-Enlightenment rationalism downplayed the tragic dimension, providing the backdrop to the myth of endless progress, and the optimism which undergirds our own culture's commitment to endless growth and consumerist paradises. Another approach would be to understand tragedy as the downfall of noble characters (such as Shakespeare's King Lear, Brutus's betrayal of Caesar). While this is an important dimension, let it not obscure the tragedy that entraps poor communities, the tragic failure of compassion at a global level, the turning-a-blind-eye to the irreparable ravaging of large tracts of the planet…

The real problem for a *theological* understanding of tragedy is that the Western classical patriarchal concept of God has to keep the being of God outside tragedy for *God to keep on being God*. But if feminist re-imaging of the divine believes in an involved and embodied God, how can God be experienced amid tragic events? What difference does divine Presence make to tragedy?

The Dilemma of Classical Theism

The dilemma is a familiar one, argued by St Augustine—and the Greek philosopher Epicurus before him—and thematized in traditional theology as theodicy. How do we understand the goodness and justice of God in the face of inexplicable, pointless suffering especially the suffering of the innocent? This is the test of faith par excellence—in Western minds at least. The argument hinges on whether the goodness of God or the power of God are to be privileged—and, as readers are aware, a torrent of novels and plays have given us anguished and poignant depictions of the dilemma, from Dostoevsky to the contemporary Jewish novelist Eli Wiesel. Wiesel, in putting God on trial, cries:

> either He dislikes his chosen people or He doesn't care about them—period. Then what has He chosen us—why not someone else for a change? Either He knows what's happening to us or He doesn't wish to know! In both cases he is... He is...guilty! Yes guilty! (Cohn-Sherbok 1989: 99).

For Wiesel, the issue is clear (one could almost say *tragically clear*): might, power—as the concepts are normally used—are seen through the lens of divine agency expressed as intervention. Yet, here, God has apparently chosen not to intervene. Can God, then, be loving?

Again, we are familiar with the solutions proffered by traditional Christianity, varying from evil seen as a result of 'privatio boni' (absence of good), to evil as a necessary component of free will, and to suffering as educating us into becoming better people (the so-called pedagogical-therapeutic explanation of Ireneus that is further developed by John Hick [1985]).

This view both depends on believing that pain and suffering do make us better people—a view strongly resisted by feminist theology—and that eschatologically, in the next world, all pain will be transformed into joy. The latter argument of course has the dangerous consequence of allowing us to explain away the full weight of suffering, where its roots lie in structural injustice. We are persuaded that this suffering is part of God's plan to test us. God promises us a greater reward for suffering nobly—borne. The tendency is still very strong to allot a spiritual meaning to suffering and to be insensitive as to who is suffering and who must take responsibility for it. It is outrageous to tell the raped Bosnian woman, the prostituted Indian child, that they should look for a spiritual meaning or that they will necessarily become better people by enduring their lot. The first step is the denunciation of what has been done to them as a crime.

If we add to this an insensitivity to race, to economic divisions of south and north, and the failure of compassion towards the victims, it is easy to see how vast amounts of suffering are allowed to coexist with an affluent Western lifestyle. The traditional Western Christian distinction between moral and physical evil further blunts this sensitivity. Moral evil—we say—is our responsibility, but earthquakes, tidal waves and tornadoes belong to the sphere of nature, and in the face of this we are helpless. It seems to me that the insensitivity to suffering and tragedy engendered by our inheriting this line of thought has distanced us from, and rendered us deaf to, the tragic voice of God in both the Hebrew Scriptures and the New Testament.

'Oh my people, what have I done to you?' cries this pain-filled God of the prophets (Mic. 6). This is the God of the anguished Jesus of Gethsemane, the desolate Jesus of Golgotha. I suggest that this is the God kept hidden by Western rationalism. My question now is: does feminist liberation theology offer a way to rediscover this hidden God in such a way as to meet God as God at the point where tragedy is encountered and experienced at the beginning of the new millennium? And could this be a way in which the mystery of this tragic God is not reduced, but experienced anew yet differently?

Encountering the Tragic God in a Post-modern World

First of all, optimism and certainty no longer characterize the twentieth century, this society that knows it holds through nuclear power and chemical weapons the key to its own annihilation. Secondly, what we thought of as clear distinctions we now realize have fuzzy, blurred boundaries. Moral and so-called natural evil are no longer so clearly separated, as we discover the part that human activity has played in ecological problems in, for example, desertification, deforestation and global warming. Even good and evil in certain situations are no longer so sharply polarized as we confront situations of ambiguity. In saying this, I do not mean that there are no acts to be condemned as completely evil, for example the wholesale slaughter of the Holocaust, and the rape of the Bosnian women. (And even if we could point to acts of heroism within these situations it would not detract from the sheer evil of what was done.) I mean to call attention to situations of choice and decision-making where *every* outcome will lead to suffering for someone. It is these kinds of situations that form the stuff of tragedy.

For example, looking to Greek tragedy, Agamemnon, king of the Greeks (in Aeschylus's trilogy, *The Oresteia*) needs a fair wind to allow his fleet to sail to try to defeat the Trojans. He is commanded by the god Apollo to sacrifice on a funeral pyre his virgin daughter Iphigeneia. What is he to do? By saving his daughter he risks defeat, and will disobey the god: to go ahead means the murder of his daughter and the loss of trust of his wife. We know that a tragic chain of events was set in motion—his own murder by his wife Clytemnestra, and the hunting of the Furies of his son, Orestes, in revenge. But the point is that this question of ambiguity has entered the moral scene.

This is even clearer in Sophocles' play, *Antigone*—and the tragedy involved here has absorbed philosophers ever since—in particular Hegel and more recently the Aristotelian philosopher, Martha Nussbaum. Here the question is that two wills, two laws, two sets of values are involved. If Antigone buries her dead brother Polyneices she disobeys the laws of the city-state. Not to do so means betrayal of—according to her—an older law, the love of kinship, the honour due to a brother, the terrible disgrace of being unburied. Nussbaum makes great play of the ambiguity involved here, pointing out how fragile is goodness (1986).

Ruprecht, however, in his book *Tragic Posture and Tragic Vision*, argues that the ambiguity has even greater tension, as it is by no means clear that we ought to privilege the position of Antigone over that of Kreon, dismissing this as a mere clinging to conventional values (Ruprecht 1994). A more contemporary dilemma would be from William Styron's film (and book) *Sophie's Choice*, where a young mother has to choose between sending her son or her daughter to the gas chambers (Styron 1979). *Sophie's Choice* is a no choice, no win situation.

The notion of ambiguity enters the arena not only in situations of decision-making where conflicting sets of values are involved, but as permeating the fragile threads of planetary existence, and this becomes a clearer through ecological and ecofeminist theory. The work of Ruth Page (1985) and the work of Sallie McFague discussed in Chapter 6 point out that the ambiguity and conflict permeating all the experiences of sentient beings, human and non-human, the chaos and unpredictability of natural phenomena, mean that a polarization of good and evil in the classical way is not helpful. For Ruth Page, it is the presence and companionship of God, and God's continuing relationship with creation that give us hope to continue:

> Yet in and through ambiguity, at every contingent place and time, among people of every age and culture, this relationship may be apprehended, God may be worshipped and all conceptions of the value and significance of experience transformed (Page 1985: 236).

As Sallie McFague suggested, when describing the ministry of Jesus as the Christic shape of the body (McFague 1993: 150) our concerns—as this Body—will focus on the needy and suffering. I would like to extend this Christic shape to tragic suffering, and see this body as wounded, flawed, arousing compassion, solidarity and leading to the creation of communities of hope.[1] This tragic suffering is also present on a cosmological plane, as McFague writes:

> Curiously, we seldom question the random effects of chance that result in good to ourselves. Few of us, for instance, ask 'Why has this good thing happened to me?' though we frequently find the world malevolent if we suffer some diminishment or reversal of fortune. Yet we cannot have one without the other. My life, your life, all life is a chance happening; so also are birth defects, cancer cells and AIDS. This brutal truth is so difficult for us to accept, that we narrow our horizon to ourselves and narrow God to a deity only concerned with my good, or at most, the good of the human species. But a cosmological, ecological perspective demands the enlargement of vision (McFague 1993: 175).

The suffering of the cosmos, the suffering of the planet—this is the enlargement of vision demanded by a cosmological perspective. But what kinds of suffering is meant by animal suffering, the suffering of every sentient being?—this is a complex issue beyond the scope of this present study.[2] What is urgent for us to consider is what it means for God as Creator to make a world where suffering and tragedy are built into the very fabric of cosmic existence.

So, it is one thing to ask questions of suffering and tragedy from a concept of God as monarchical and distant from the world (classical theism), seeing divine agency as *interventionist* (as described above), and divine power as coercive; it is another to ask it from a belief in God as present to and grieving with us (the *organic, embodied* model), as we struggle with our grief:

1. This is the concern of my book, *The Outrageous Pursuit of Hope* (Grey 2000).
2. See, however, the theme articles in Grey (ed.) 1995.

> In the organic model we are with God whether we live or die, for
> whether our bodies are alive or return to the other form of embodiment
> from which they came, they are within the Body of God (McFague
> 1993: 176).

This insight moves us forward, if we can understand and accept that this
particular world could not be structured any differently: that all this
glorious mix of creativity, chance, randomness could not be otherwise,
and the price of complexity and intensity of experience is capacity for
pain. (This is not to collapse everything into a *no pain, no gain* theology.)
But what is still unexplained is how to give meaning to the power of
God in the midst of suffering and tragedy. If God suffers with us, does
the concept of a powerful God have any meaning at all? And, secondly,
even if there is another way to understand the power of God (instead of
being extrinsic and coercive), even if God suffers with us, is this the only
answer to the tragic dimension? That is, *no answer...just suffer...that's how
it is...*

God's Power as the Power of Compassion

So the next stage in the argument is to shift from the very restricted idea
of God's power as 'might', as intervening arbitrarily with the laws of
nature, normally understood through a military analogy, towards seeing
how a different kind of power works in real situations of suffering.[3]

The feminist theologian Wendy Farley based a theodicy on the idea
of God's power as the power of compassion (1990). Compassion for her
is not a feeling but a relational mode. It is an enduring disposition which
integrates many dimensions into a coherent model of world-engage-
ment, as the whole self becomes a servant of compassion's care for the
world:

> Compassion [for Farley] is not a one-sided, paternalistic pity, but is a form
> of love, the disposition to love in a world filled with suffering, always
> respecting the integrity of the other. Compassion is the power that drives
> to justice, beyond the narrow limits of a legalism which contents itself
> with punishing the wicked...it is a 'power to bring to life what is broken
> by pain, to bring to justice and redemption what is twisted by brutality'[4]
> (Grey 1993: 115).

---

3.   I am aware that Process thought sees divine power as coercive and persua-
sive, referring to the 'lure of God'.

4.   Here I develop some of Wendy Farley's ideas.

Farley's argument—which I have developed—does explain how suffering people do experience the power and love of God. This is a God who 'hears the cry of the poor' as the Hebrew psalms say. God's power as compassionate love is also a model par excellence for a pastoral response of human beings towards each other in situations of suffering. What else is there to do but practise compassion?

But this does not solve the question of the tragic dimension, of the unanswered cry, of the total weight of innocent, meaningless suffering, the brutality that seizes a whole society *en bloc*. What is more, it hints that *all* suffering can be redeemed by God's compassion, when the tragic dimension suggests that this is precisely the issue. All suffering *cannot* be redeemed—in earthly life, at least.

Could there even be tragedy caught up in the divine nature itself, as is hinted by the text of Isaiah 40, 'I am God: I create weal and woe…'? Could it be, perhaps, in not giving attention to this question, that the debate—in Western Christian thinking at least—remains locked in impasse?

Tragedy in the Hidden Heart of God?

I have hinted already that Christian theology's insistence that pure goodness alone constitutes God's nature, a goodness that is totally opposed to every suggestion of evil, yet historically opposed to the Gnostic view that physicality and matter are tainted, is itself problematic. Increasingly we have been challenged to discover *the dark side of God*—a phrase itself tinged with racism—and given analogies from other cosmologies where God is not totally good. Secondly, since Jurgen Moltmann's *The Crucified God* (1974), there has been a growing strand in theology understanding God as involved with our pain and linking with a more Jewish understanding of the pain of God.[5]

What I now develop is a deepening of this strand from feminist and ecofeminist theological thought in many contexts. Unsurprisingly, the exploration emerges from world-views based on experience of poor, suffering women: this suffering is frequently linked with the earth (as the well-being of women and earth are inextricably intermingled). If we add to this, that the earth is understood as the Body of God, then God is involved in earth suffering at a very profound level.

5.   See discussion in Chapter 4, *God—our Passion for Justice*.

This, Wendy Farley would describe as the tragic element in the divine being:

> divine love is tragic in the more profound sense that it addresses suffering within a context that it created itself. A theology of divine love finds itself in a similar position to theologies of sovereignty: both in the end must attribute the existence of evil to God (1990: 107).

There are differing reactions to this: process theology, for example, does not understand God as creating from nothing *(ex nihilo)*, thus allowing complexity in the continual creativity from chaos, *tehom*. I have suggested above that we simply have to accept that we do not know if God could have created any *different* kind of world. Even those we imagine through science fiction, overturning gender categories, creating cyborgs and monsters, are all conceptually linked with our thinking powers derived from this world. So, if God is totally involved with the tragic, what needs to be understood is what difference it makes: if God cannot eradicate tragedy, make it less tragic and bearable, does belief in God add anything? Should we simply bow to the inevitable?

One important response is made by the feminist theologian, Kathleen Sands. She is strong in her critique of theology and feminist theology in particular for neglecting or too easily passing over the tragic dimension. But the foundation of her critique is particularly crucial: Sands argues that tragedy is the moral paradox that beings who want goodness cannot remain uncontaminated by evil:

> The religious and moral risk of tragic consciousness…is to encounter elemental power/truth in its radical plurality, unmooring the good from any metaphysical anchor, so that it becomes an entirely human, entirely fragile relationship (Sands 1994: 63).

The main thrust of her critique of feminist theologians who do take tragedy seriously—and the two she takes as examples are Rosemary Radford Ruether and Carol Christ, the former a Catholic Christian and the second a post-Christian thealogian of goddess spirituality[6]—is the assertion of a goodness beyond tragedy, an absolute goodness which will, in the end, triumph over tragedy. This is a typical assertion of Christian theology. As Nicholas Lash wrote: 'In the end, God heals absolutely. But we work in the meantime' (Lash 1991: 61).

First of all, Sands criticizes Rosemary Ruether, because in her search for justice and identification of sin as injustice, she relegates finitude and

---

6. See the discussion in Chapter 2.

mortality to the realm of the tragic and thus can only have attributes of God as Absolute Freedom, and transcendent Truth by conceiving a 'reality not bound by the conditions of time and space' (Sands 1994: 93). But, says Sands, recognizing our fragility and vulnerability means living *without* such metaphysical guarantees:

> cosmic eggs have only the fragile nests of social and biotic community in which to hatch (110).

For her, the continuing power and persuasiveness of feminist theology

> will depend much less on whether we have theoretical answers to evil than on whether we 'know the dance' that goes with the moral discern- ment in our places and moments (69).

But neither—for Sands—does the work of Carol Christ provide a way forward. Carol Christ's latest book, *Rebirth of the Goddess* (1997) (see Chapter 2), now understands the Goddess as the fragile web of life, the interdependence of all sentient and organic life. The power or energy of eros, desire, energizes and is at the heart of the process, an eros that unites spiritual and social quests. This is a thoroughly immanent, ecological understanding of female deity with links with Process thought (the Goddess is understood as in relationship with all becoming), and with some traditional liberal theology (for example, Paul Tillich), since the Goddess is the ground of all being. Sands, although in agreement with much of Christ's work, objects to the new absolute or metaphysical prin- ciple found in it, 'goodness at the heart of nature', as well as to the cen- trality of eros. Given that eros is defined as 'the passion to connect', it is by no means clear that it can play this idealized role of connecting vio- lated and oppressed peoples the world over with their deepest desires.[7]

The way forward in Sands's opinion is trying to live in the ruins of the Absolutes, without their closure, in the collapsing of the patriarchal paradise. She concludes,

> Out here, beyond the walls of paradise, not only are the colours brighter, and hardest to match, but the fabrics of our truths, beauties and goods is always unravelling. Were our hopes to rely on perfect beginnings and ends, this would surely be cause for despair. But if hope, instead, is our messy, multiform continuance, then what we need is rather to mourn and laugh and dance until our flesh remembers how the world goes on (Sands 1994: 169).

---

7.   A similar argument was used in the preceding chapter in connection with the work of Carter Heyward.

What seems right in this approach is that we are always suspended between tragedy and hope: that they are alternate sides of the same coin. And, as Mercy Amba Oduyoye has written, 'African women wear hope like a skin' (Oduyoye 2001). But, whether we use the metaphor of 'joining the dance', the ethical stance of 'praxis of compassion', of honouring the Body of God, the fragile web of life, this still does not answer the question of God. In the ruins of the Absolutes, the refusal to foreclose on resolving the tragic, has God been written out of the text? And if there are no solutions to tragedy, what is the substance of hope?

I explore now a few pointers as to a way forward, pointers to be taken further in the next chapter. First, given all that we know about chaos, unpredictability, messiness and ambiguity, it could be that, as Peter Schaeffer in his play *Equus* wrote, we are given 'a way of seeing in the dark', not an end to darkness. And, as Christians, our way of seeing is through commitment to the basic narrative of Christianity. In fact, Ruprecht's *Tragic Vision* (1994) ends with a tragic reading of Jesus in Gethsemane:

> Mark's Jesus comes bearing two things: good news and hard sayings. Only by dwelling with the negative—the suffering and the hardness of life—may the good news be appreciated for what it is. It could almost be said that a sincere faith in the resurrection makes dwelling with the Crucified practically impossible. If you know how a story ends, you never hear its beginning or its middle the same way... Mark's Gospel makes a tragic kind of sense. His warning reverberates through the corridors of time and speaks to us still, if we have the ears and the eyes and the stomach for it. Dwell within the negative, and face the horror of crucifixions, the awful sense of abandonment in the Garden and the cross. 'The Lord is not here' (227-28).

We cannot, he argues, trade in our destiny for a mess of pottage (228). But this still does not answer how God's power actually does work. Light has to be shed through understanding this *non-coercively*, as compassion and empathy, yes, but also as linked with God's vulnerability, with what Sarah Coakley has described as the paradox of power and vulnerability in God (Coakley 1996).[8]

In an insightful discussion of the *kenosis* of Jesus, she both raises the question for feminism that there are other ways of confronting fragility, suffering and 'self-emptying' than in the language of victimhood; and the question that for God, the only way for power to be exercised is in

---

8. This is developed in her forthcoming book, *God, Sexuality and the Self*.

that utter transparency of vulnerability that Jesus underwent in Gethsemane, because this is the place of the self's transformation and entering
into God. Openness to divine power is precisely through the vulnerability that God and humanity share with the processes of sentient life.

In a completely different context, the Jewish victim of Auschwitz,
Etty Hillesum, grasped the power of human vulnerability as something
to be used for God's longing for peace and reconciliation. She wrote:

> Alas, there doesn't seem very much You yourself can do about our cir-
> cumstances, our lives... You cannot help us but we must help You to
> defend Your dwelling place inside us to the last... (Hillesum 1985: 187).

> Sometimes they (people) seem to me like houses with open doors. I walk
> in and roam through passages and rooms, and every house is furnished a
> little differently and yet they are all of them the same, and every one must
> be turned into a dwelling for you O God. And I promise you, yes, I
> promise that I shall try to find a dwelling for you in as many houses as
> possible... Please forgive this poor metaphor (215).

And we are speaking here about a woman, who laughingly described
herself as 'the girl who couldn't pray' and who, in the end, before her
death, wanted to be nothing else other than the 'praying heart of the
concentration camp', refusing to allow hatred for the persecutors to be
the last word. Sarah Coakley argues that it is in prayer, in contemplative,
wordless prayer that 'we ourselves enact, or enter into...the unique
intersection of vulnerable, "non-grasping" humanity and divine power,
itself "made perfect in weakness"' (Coakley 1996: 110).

But what she calls the *hiatus* of expectant waiting, I want to call a very
active stance. It is expectant waiting, and it is this hope that energizes
Christic communities to keep on 'seeing in the dark'. But it is a waiting
filled with faith, hope and Spirit-filled compassionate love. And in
Mark's Gospel it is the biblical women who embody this. To return to
Gethsemane: while the Synoptics depict the apostles as falling asleep,
thus increasing the desolation of Jesus, in the cells of the Monastery of
San Marco in Florence is a fresco of Fra Angelico, showing Martha and
the community of women at the gates of Gethsemane, watching and
praying. It was also a woman who anointed Jesus in full consciousness of
what was to come (Mk 14), and the three women who watched the
crucifixion were—apparently—the same three at the tomb on Resurrection morning.

So, instead of looking for a metaphysical solution and end to the
tragic dimension, if we look to the resources of the faith communities of

prayer, solidarity and action—perhaps the Christian community's equivalent of Sands's *joining the dance*?—we discover that it is there—but not only there—that the presence of God has been promised and to be trusted, empowering and transforming, hearing our laments, screams of grief and even our wordless cries, vulnerable with our vulnerability, promising us—not an end to darkness and tragedy—but pouring out light within it. But for that to furnish 'a way of seeing in the dark' we have to follow the path of Sophia, wisdom: and it is in Sophia that we might find a grounding image for a feminist naming of God.

Chapter Eight

The Re-emergence of Sophia

Fairest Sophia, Ruler of all nature,
Thou in whom earth and heav'n are one,
Thee will I cherish, Thee will I honor,
Thou, my soul's glory, joy and crown
(Cole, Ronan and Taussig 1996: 185).

In the figure of Sophia many strands of feminist theological thinking on God converge. Sophia returns at a time when there has been a growing enthusiasm for a renewal of a Spirit theology. This needs to be understood historically: it is well-accepted that in the Western church there has been an over-concentration on Christology, and feminist theology has frequently documented the absolutist, political tendencies this has caused (Ruether 1983; Schüssler Fiorenza 1995). Since the growth of the charismatic movement in the late sixties, the mushrooming of house-churches, and the more recent phenomena of the Toronto Blessing, the success of the Alpha movement and the spread of Pentecostalism (see Porter and Richter 1995; Cox 1997), new movements of the Holy Spirit are certainly changing the face of the Church as a whole.[1] But it is the hope of discovering a God not imaged as essentially male that has inspired some of the feminist theological recovery of the Spirit. What is striking, however, is the way that feminist thinkers resist the rather crude attempts to identify the Spirit as female, in order—it is supposed—to give women some kind of link to the Trinitarian God. Hence, Leonardo Boff (1989) had attempted—with what Sarah Coakley has called

---

1.   Clearly there are many issues here, beyond the scope of this study, such as the political links in the different forms of charismatic movements, the authoritarian nature of some of the forms of leaderships, the authenticity of some of the healing movements, as well as the cult nature of some of the manifestations.

'unreconstructed Jungianism'!—to make an ontological link between women—Mary, mother of Jesus—and the Holy Spirit, whereas men are directly linked with Jesus (Coakley 1992). There were, of course, earlier attempts to describe the Holy Spirit with female imagery, referring principally to the writings of Ephrem the Syrian (Coakley 1988). The reason for the objections to identifying the Spirit as feminine—quite apart from the lack of weight to this in the tradition—is that it would seem to allocate a token presence of the female within the divine, as well as restricting the female representation in the Trinity to the Spirit. Thus Sarah Coakley cites (critically) Yves Congar, who is also inclined to understand Holy Spirit as female. The problem is that to identify the Spirit with such roles as 'comforting', 'mothering', 'nurturing', both latches on to an essentialist view of female-ness, and leaves God the Father in a masculine, patriarchal world, reinforcing its symbolism. But contemporary thinking wants to redeem masculinity as to liberate femininity![2] Feminist theology rather wants to rediscover the richness and diversity of the role of the Spirit in creation, in relationships, in empowering prophetic movements and in resisting all kinds of oppressive structures, in as full a manner as possible. The Spirit as the power of truth is the inspiration. Thus, Elizabeth Johnson writes of Hildegarde of Bingen's imaging of the Spirit:

> The Spirit [Hildegarde writes] is the life of all creatures, the way in which everything is penetrated with connectedness and relatedness; a burning fire who sparks, ignites, inflames, kindles hearts; a guide in the fog; a balm for wounds; a shining serenity; an overflowing fountain that spreads to all sides. She is life, movement, color, radiance, restorative stillness in the din. Her power makes all withered sticks and souls green again with the juice of life. She purifies, absolves, strengthens, heals, gathers the per-plexed, seeks the lost. She pours the juice of contrition into hardened hearts. She plays music in the soul, being herself the melody of praise and joy. She awakens mighty hope, blowing everywhere the winds of renewal in creation (Johnson 1994: 127-28).

Building on this broadened notion of Spirit, when feminist theologians speak of Sophia, we can begin to see the link—but not identification—between the roles of Spirit and Sophia. This means speaking of Spirit-Sophia in the context of a Trinitarian God. Texts like Wis. 7.22-23, 27 have already made this link:

---

2.   See the discussion of this in Ianthe Pratt (1997).

> There is in her a spirit that is intelligent, holy,
> unique, manifold, subtle,
> mobile, clear, unpolluted,
> distinct, invulnerable, loving the good, keen,
> irresistible, beneficent, humane,
> steadfast, sure, free from anxiety,
> all-powerful, overseeing all…
>
> Although she is but one, she can do all things,
> and whole remaining in herself, she renews all things,
> in every generation she passes into holy souls
> and makes them friends of God and prophets (Wis. 7.22-23, 27).

Before exploring what this means, I first want to convey the flavour of the inspiration of Sophia/Wisdom in feminist theological circles—with the underlying question, 'Who is Sophia?' kept well in mind. Capturing the unarticulated depths that Wisdom tries to reach, the late—and much-loved—Nelle Morton wrote:

> Wisdom is Feminist and suggests an experience earlier than a word (Morton 1985: 175).[3]

The theologian Lucy Tatman, in the recent dictionary, *An A to Z of Feminist Theology*, writes, imaginatively, that

> Once upon a time there was Wisdom. There was Wisdom and she was present everywhere with all the intensity and all the desire of all there was. And once the Word was spoken she and she alone dived into the spaces between the words, blessing the silence out of which new worlds were born. Now, as it was in the beginning, Wisdom is hearing all creation into speech (Tatman 1996: 236).

Already we are given the impression that Wisdom speaks to an experience deeper than words, touches the imagination, and has mythological significance. And we cannot ignore the ironical, whimsical play of Mary Daly in her iconoclastic *Wickedary*: here Wisdom becomes *Whizzdom*, the elemental spinning into new, creative space, as a-mazing Amazon, reaching into elemental meta-memory, time and origins (Daly and Caputi 1988: 154).

What I try now to do here is to sketch a kind of cartography for Sophia, Lady Wisdom, weaving in and out of the many inspirational strands in which she is sought and savoured, without ignoring the negative reactions and backlash she has evoked and the theological issues

---

3.   A helpful resource for this section have been several articles from *Feminist Theology* (1997).

raised. First, Sophia appears in the Wisdom literature of the Hebrew Bible: she is always imaged as divine female—hence the reams of literature evoked on Sophia as feminine or feminist face of God. But why did Sophia come comparatively late into the biblical literature? (She does not appear at all in the Pentateuch, the five books of Moses.) One suggestion is that she enters at a moment, namely, the loss of the monarchy, when the prophets were inviting the Jewish people to understand the mercy of God in a more universalist way—beyond the narrow confines of their own people. Hence the imagery of Sophia setting a table, summoning people to the feast from the highways and byways (Prov. 9; Isa. 55) followed by the New Testament imagery of the messianic banquet. Elizabeth Schüssler Fiorenza has suggested that

> the change from a monarchic, centrally-administrated society to a society oriented towards the needs and interests of families and extended households was positively expressed in the image of the ideal Israelite woman in Proverbs 31 and in the praise of Woman Wisdom who builds her cosmic house (Proverbs 9) (Schüssler Fiorenza 1995: 134).

The Swiss scholar, Silvia Schroer, suggests that what the figure of Sophia-Wisdom does is to integrate masculine and feminine elements into the image of God and to connect such an 'inclusive monotheism' with the experience of women in Israel (Schroer 1991), but that this would be replaced by a new alliance of temple, priesthood and law that became less open to women.

Wisdom imagery, too, has implications for our own context: the sheer poetic power of the imagery of the biblical Sophia grips us—as well as evoking questions as to why she could have been forgotten or marginalized by the dominant tradition and what implications she has for the complex questions of today. As Schüssler Fiorenza wrote:

> How can we trace the spoor of divine Sophia in biblical writings in such a way that the theological possibilities offered by Wisdom, the divine Woman of Justice, but never quite realised in history, can be realised? (Schüssler Fiorenza 1995: 133).

Sophia is *creative energy* with God at the dawn of creation (Prov. 7; Eccl. 24.3-5). She is *Teacher* (Prov. 8.1-11). Sometimes she is *both Teacher and what is taught* (Prov. 4.5, 8). To fall in love with Sophia is to fall in love with Wisdom itself. And she can *be lover, mother and Teacher* all at the same time (Eccl. 4.11-16). Yet, too, she has an organic link with creation, imaged as *tree and plant* (Eccl. 24.12-19).[4] Sophia dwells in Israel, and celebrates festive liturgies in the temple, 'sends prophets, apostles and wise people, and makes those who follow her friends of God' (Schüssler Fiorenza 1995: 135). In fact, making people friends of God is characteristic of the activity of Sophia, as Elizabeth Johnson points out:

> To see God and the world existing in a relationship of friendship, each indwelling the other, has deep infinity with women's experience. It also corresponds to several key biblical themes. Wisdom's path is one, for a characteristic activity of Sophia is friend-making: 'From generation unto generation she passes into holy souls and makes them friends of God, and prophets' (Wis. 7.27) (Johnson 1994: 235).

Secondly, alongside this strand from Jewish scriptures I place the *mythological* strand, and the role of Sophia in other ancient Near Eastern cultures. For Sophia is also a goddess figure appearing in the religions and cosmologies of many lands. She may be associated with Isis of Egypt, Ishtar-Astarte of Mesopotamia and Babylon, Asherah-Ashteroth of the Canaanite religion—all of whom are very much in the background of the biblical imagery. Some would even consider the woman clothed with the sun of Revelations 12 to be a figure of Sophia and linked with Isis:

> The connections between Isis and Sophia are very significant and show us Sophia's strongest links to the ancient Goddess tradition. Isis is a Saviour goddess par excellence, one who combines the elements of the Black Goddess and the Hellenic philosophies which went to create the definitive Sophia (Matthews 1991: 65).

Sophia has been compared with Isis through her role in saving her people (Wis. 10.9), through the events selected to illustrate this role, and through the 'allusive re-telling of these events in such a way that they resonate with the mythic pattern of the Isis-Horus cycle' (Kloppenborg 1982: 72).

As the Canaanite goddess Asherah, Sophia was even considered to be Yahweh's consort (Long 1992). Asphodel Long sums up this tradition:

> That the Hebrews worshipped a 'queen of heaven' is fully attested, and this queen of heaven is well-known throughout the Ancient Near East and Hellenistic world. In becoming the consort of Yahweh, Asherah remained a personified goddess with her own praxis, and the queen of Heaven was autonomous in her own right. The two may not be identified with each other (1992: 136).

---

4.   For a fuller account, see Cole, Ronan and Taussig (1996).

Sophia has also been identified with the earth mother goddess of Greece and Rome, as well as with the eastern mother goddesses, Durga of Hinduism for example, and the Celtic mother goddesses. As such she is a powerful inspiration to the Goddess movement today—as was explored in Chapter 2—and is extensively portrayed as Goddess of Wisdom in the work of Caitlin Matthews (1991), for example, who links such diverse images of Sophia as 'the Black Virgin', with 'The Grail Goddess' and 'Virgo Viriditas'.

The fascination and absorption with Sophia today is that for many she fills the empty hole of having no female imaginary of the divine. But in the anthropocentric, patriarchal context in which she first appeared within Judaism and Christianity this was not a high priority. It has to be admitted that in the secular atmosphere of Solomon's court—where many think Wisdom traditions originated—the position of women was a subordinate one. In most of the texts women are conspicuous by absence. There was no overt connection made between Sophia and the position of ordinary women. What we are doing today is to create this link.

But these historical circumstances may well have contributed to the disappearance of Sophia from the Tradition. One of the main causes of this must be the way that the Jewish writer Philo identified Sophia-Wisdom with the Logos, the son of God, who, in John's Gospel became 'The Word made flesh'. Although Philo did use mythological-cosmological imagery to express the psychological realities of the human soul, this replacement of Sophia with Logos-Israel, writes Schussler Fiorenza, 'produced the masculine linguistic sequence *Father-Son of G*d, Sons of the G*d*' (Schüssler Fiorenza 1995: 138, italics in original). Asphodel Long expresses it from a Jewish perspective:

> With the advent of Christianity, the notion of female Wisdom was subsumed into Jesus Christ, subsequently into the Third Person of the Trinity, the holy Spirit, and eventually into 'Mother Church'. Although in the last two named some semblance of the female remained attached for a while, the Christian religion in all its various forms became totally male-dominated, with the Church acting as bulwark of male supremacy (Long 1992: 139).

Hence the importance of the project of Fiorenza in reclaiming a Wisdom Christology: but this wisdom is a liberating Wisdom where Jesus, as Sophia's messenger and prophet, has a mission to proclaim God's Kingdom to the poor and dispossessed.[5]

But the challenge in the re-imagining is that Sophia, even though divine, must not be allowed to lose touch with real women in their struggles. This links with the *third strand* which is the way that Sophia as goddess functions as an empowering figure in women's spiritual journey. The work of Carol Christ encapsulates this best, as she depicts her own journey from the experience of *no identity*, of being 'no-thing' in traditional Christian spirituality, to discovering the goddess as a powerful symbol of the divine female (see Chapter 2). Sophia can be the image of a strong, wise woman, ageing, elderly or old, thus liberating women from enslavement to fashion, the idealizing of youth and slimness, and the fear and revulsion of old age and death. As such, Sophia as Wise Woman has appeared in female Trinities, for example, the Celtic Trinity, consisting of the young girl, the Mother and the Crone.

From these last two strands it is clear that the inspiration of Sophia is much wider than the Jewish and Christian traditions. So, when I add the *fourth* strand to this map, namely Sophia in Christian feminist liturgies, it is understandable why there has been so much negative reaction, even backlash, from some traditional Christian circles. The Swedish scholar Ninna Beckman, in her *Sophia* article in *Feminist Theology* (Beckman 1997) cites rich and diverse Christian feminist liturgies in the United States, the creative liturgies of her own Swedish context, and the experience of the Women's Synod in Gmünden, Austria, 1996. Here, she describes the image of Sophia arising—it would seem—spontaneously across a range of liturgies and speeches. This included my own keynote speech, on personal development, which I had entitled (unaware of the role that Sophia would play in the Synod as a whole), 'Empowered to Lead: Sophia's Daughters Blaze a Trail' (Grey 1997c: 91-106). But it was the 'Re-imagining' Conference of the WCC in Minneapolis, 1993, which sparked off the most bitter reactions and charges of heresy—despite the fact that the evaluation of the participants of 'Re-Imagining' was almost unanimously positive. To give an indication of the fury evoked, this is an example from an editorial of the *Presbyterian Layman* (27 January 1994):

> In Minneapolis the Word of God incarnate was rejected as too limiting and confining for women—so, Christ was replaced with Christa, Sophia and other assorted Goddesses; the canon of Scripture was unilaterally reopened; and the chief proclamation was that since we were already

5.   Schüssler Fiorenza wants to link the empty tomb tradition associated with women, as originating in this understanding of Jesus as Sophia's prophet.

gods, we effect our own salvation when we look within ourselves and affirm our own divinity (Beckman 1997: 42).

A similar fury was incurred—Beckman relates—by Sophia services in the Church of Sweden. Whereas it is not the purpose in this study to plunge into a wholesale exegesis of the 'Re-imagining' event, it is important to note here that what is at stake in the furious rejection of Sophia images is the threat to traditional male imagery of God being upheld by the both latent and blatant misogyny of the Christian tradition as well as the implications new images bring for a changed social order. Must it be inevitable that in trying to change this order, that the charge of heresy and paganism will always be incurred?

This is why at this point I weave two more specifically Christian strands into the web. Fifth, Sophia is also present in the Russian Orthodox theological tradition, especially in the works of Pavel Florensky, Vladimir Soloviev and Sergei Bulgakov. For Bulgakov (as Celia Deane-Drummond tells us in her article on Sophia [1997]), Sophiology is a way of interpreting all theology, not just a theology of creation:

> The future of living Christianity rests with the Sophianic interpretation of the world and of its destiny. All the dogmatic problems of modern Christian dogmatic and ascetics seem to form a kind of knot, the unravelling of which inevitably leads to Sophiology. For this reason in the true sense, of the word, Sophiology is a theology of *crisis*, not of distinction, but of salvation (Sergei Bulgakov in Deane-Drummond 1997: 16 [italics original]).

Moreover, Bulgakov, she writes (1997: 29), 'recognised that Sophia has a "shadow side" which faces up to evil in the universe'. The Cross assumes a unique role in this theology, becoming the place of crucifixion of all creation, not just suffering humanity. Thus, she suggests, not only the shocking image of the Christa is suggested by Sophia, crucified, but the radical image of crucified nature.

Hence, I would add, God as Sophia is another face of the embodiment of God, another manifestation of God's vulnerability in the world —the female, but not only the female, as the vulnerable face of God— and a manifestation of how tragedy is caught up into God. It is interesting to note that the late Thomas Merton, the Trappist monk, was fascinated by the image of Sophia—which he discovered from Russian sources: God enters creation as Sophia—and he understood Lara in Dr Zhivago as one of these figures (Carr 1988: 71). It is tempting to muse how, if Merton had lived, this understanding of God as Sophia would have developed.

But it was the prophetic understanding of Sophia as crisis, judgment, discernment, which I was invoking in my book, *The Wisdom of Fools?* (Grey 1993). There the figure of Sophia invokes a myth of connected living, non-dualist, ecological, justice-centred and relational. I opposed this to the Logos myth, which encapsulates much of the current ethos of society as competitive, materialistic, success-oriented and individualistic. This proposal of Sophia as metaphor critiquing culture is my fifth strand. Celia Deane-Drummond herself proposes Sophia as a metaphor for an ecological theology. She builds on the scriptural themes of wisdom and creative energy, as well as integrating transcendent and immanent wisdom, understanding both as coming from God and coming from the earth (Deane-Drummond 1997). In a recent presentation she has suggested that the metaphor of Sophia-Wisdom is one to be called on for the development of science, suggesting that deeper values than mere technological sophistication need to be invoked (Deane-Drummond 1998). Sophia-Wisdom—for example, in an issue like genetically-modified food, looks to an eschatology of the future of the world in God: this acts as a critique of the present, of all short-term solutions damaging to earth and people alike.

The last—and sixth—strand I will introduce is the steadily insistent way that feminist theology has been working on the integrating of scriptural Sophia themes within Christian doctrine and systematic theology. Thus, Elizabeth Johnson, weaving a Trinitarian theology around the notion of Wisdom–Sophia, does not re-inscribe female characteristics on a father-God, but rather tries to transform and enrich our idea of monotheism:

> God is God as Spirit-Sophia, the mobile, pure, people-loving Spirit who pervades every wretched corner, wailing at the waste, releasing power that enables fresh starts. Her energy quickens the earth to life, her beauty shines in the stars, her strength breaks forth in every fragment of shalom and renewal that transpires in arenas of violence and meaninglessness... Sophia-God dwells in the world at its center and at its edges, an active vitality crying out in labour, birthing the new creation. Fire, wind, water and the color purple are her signs (Johnson 1994 esp. pp. 191-223).

Similarly, the authors of *Wisdom's Feast* (Cole, Ronan and Taussig 1996), on the basis of the biblical material, develop Sophia traditions for creative liturgy and ritual in an imaginative fashion.

A rich weave—these six strands! And indeed they come together in the way that divine Sophia-Wisdom challenges the mighty from their seats, and privileges the little ones in the contemporary world. Sophia offers a prophetic challenge to culture's idolatry of power, military force and money. A clue comes from the American feminist, Catherine Keller when she refers to wisdom as 'trickster', this 'spider-spirit of wisdom' which might subvert the worldwide web of power and knowledge (Keller 1996: 308).[6] She is referring to an extraordinary cosmic wisdom figure from a mysterious little text, 'The Thunder, Perfect Mind' unearthed with many of the so-called 'lost Gospels' at Nag Hammadi: this quotation seems to evoke an iconoclastic figure, refusing to be boxed in by any Western dualistic structure:

> For I am the first and the last.
> I am the honoured one and the scorned one.
> I am the whore and the holy one.
> I am the wife and the virgin.
> I am the mother and the daughter…
> I am the barren one and many are her sons.
> I am she whose wedding is great,
> and I have not taken a husband.
> I am the silence that is incomprehensible
> And the idea whose remembrance is frequent (cited in Keller 1996: 308).

Does this paradoxical wisdom, subversive, mocking the system, perhaps open up a critique of the conventional motions of cleverness and intelligence (an idea already hinted at by Celia Deane-Drummond)? I believe this is one of the main reasons why we are witnessing the re-emergence of Sophia as figure of the divine for our times.

For we live in times that cry out for genuine wisdom instead of bombardment with information; for authentic communication and communion instead of shallow sound-bites; for a valuing of the knowledge from the grassroots, instead of enforced knowledge from on high; and for the recovery of wisdom and pride in ancient knowledge of culturally marginal groups. This is the mission of Sophia. For example, in the desert of Rajasthan, N. India, the ancient ways of coping in times of water shortage have been 'forgotten': it is true that modern demands mean that the water supply is inadequate for the present excessive demand. But these rural people have also been made to feel inadequate, 'primitive', and uneducated in the face of Western, urban, educated technology. *Sophia wisdom* empowers such communities to recover both their ancient knowledge and their confidence in traditional ways. Sophia

---

6. The paradoxes of trickster imagery are traced by Camp (1995).

wisdom is a *connecting wisdom*, that does not despise practical skills (in Aristotle's terms, *phronesis*), and honours the communal re-membering of disinherited communities. This is the wisdom of the 'raging Stoic grandmother' (Rich 1978: 66), the young child, the fools and clowns, of those who dare to live up trees and down tunnels to save the country-side. Thus for Sophia, connecting wisdom is ecological wisdom, this, too, often residing with country people who respect the rhythm of the seasons and the ecology of their local habitat. Pastoral practice and psychotherapy both now respect ecological wisdom and relationship with nature as part of their method (Clinebell 1996).

But this book is about images of God, and the remarkable feature about the re-emergence of Sophia is the creative life she inspires in lovers of God. Sophia as Wise Woman is seen as the one who weaves a quilt from the fragments of women's lives. She inspires the Dance of Wisdom, 'Weaving Wisdom's Circle' as June Boyce-Tillman puts it in her music (Boyce-Tillman 1996: 24). She is the muse of poets and artists, of solitary contemplatives and the heart and soul of community, inspiring both silence and joyous celebration. Sophia-Wisdom encourages us to overcome boundaries and to make connections with all wisdom seekers and pilgrims. But it is as old Wise Woman, who heals the bruised bodies of violated women, as wise African women, as the powerful mothers of Guatemala who kept the family together throughout the war, as the Irish women of Peace—these are Sophia images of our times. They are the communities of women who give mutual strength and forge a new unity in difference. As one woman put it:

> I felt so at one with these women from all over the world. That oneness was felt in the sacred presence that permeated the room where we gathered and in the stories we heard and told each other at our tables (Beckman 1997: 53).

Hence Sophia's power is experienced in connecting with wisdom traditions in many faiths, and with wisdom cosmologies kinder to creation than those in the West (Berry 1999: 176-95). Although Sophia as Hochmah and then as Christ, Sophia's prophet, belongs to the deepest well-springs of tradition, yet she flourishes anew as divine epiphany for our times:

> Sophia, Sophia, spring up within our hearts,
> Sophia, Sophia, discern in us your truth.
> Sophia, Sophia, bring wisdom to our souls (Boyce-Tillman 1996: 23).

Epilogue

The Journey is Home[1]

For me is God not so much a dimension as a Voice who summons me, as much from deep within myself as from outside, from creation. Everywhere in creation you perceive the 'vestigia Dei', the traces of God, as it were *the footsteps of God*, if you let yourself be touched by them. For me evolution has become a source of new clarity; in the previous development of all that has life, a sharpening and refinement of consciousness has grown in humanity: this brought an attunement with the mystery of God. As soon as humanity existed this could be revealed in the ancient religions, in nature religions, in the Hebrew bible and in the New Testament.

Catherina Halkes, *Sterven om te Leven*[2]

A book with such a subject as this can have no real end. The mystery of God has such profundity that to pretend that a small study can be comprehensive is an absurdity. The apophatic tradition,[3] the *Via Negativa*, silence in the face of the mystery of God—these dimensions could stand in sharp critique of all that has been said here. And yet the very inexhaustibility of this mystery admits the possibility of new imagery, new naming, fresh and startling experiences of the divine. As Catharina Halkes has said, in the above-quoted passage, the traces of the sacred are all around, permeating the totality of experience. Our perceptions on the other hand, so limited, can still be awakened to fresh and illuminating dimensions. Such has been the nature of this attempt—simply to present aspects of this new naming from voices not usually part of the mainstream Christian tradition.[4]

1. This is the title of Nelle Morton's book (1985).
2. *Dying to Live* (translation, M. Grey).
3. Literally, 'unspeakable'. The tradition that nothing can be asserted about God, is a strong mystical tradition.
4. That is, apart from a few mystics like Julian of Norwich and Hildegarde of Bingen.

Nor is it possible to place this process of discovering new images of God into careful, systematic categories (even if chapters must have titles). By definition, the mystery of God is open-ended and must resist all closure. Secondly, throughout this book I have stressed diversity and faithfulness to context as part of the feminist theological enterprise. So there can be no neat tidying up at the end of the endeavour. What follows therefore, are personal reflections and indications of future directions, reflections which inevitably suffer from the limitations of my own situation.

Mary, Female Face of the Divine?

Some will have wondered why there has been no systematic treatment of Mary of Nazareth as representing the female face of God. Now that there is such great interest in Mariology, there was no need here to focus on Mary as such in a book about God.[5] Secondly, there have been many misconceptions over the role of Mary. Roman Catholics have often been misconstrued as worshipping Mary in a way only appropriate for God. This is a two-edged sword: official theology has always been clear that *latria,* worship, was given only to the divine. Honour and devotion have always been given to Mary as mother of Jesus, Son of God. Yet, frequently it has seemed that this led to many excesses. There is also an area of great ambiguity here for women. At times in history when God seemed remote—and far removed from the struggles of women—Mary was comfortingly near. Mary was always the guarantee that Jesus was human as well as divine. 'Through Mary to Jesus', as the popular saying went. At times and in certain cultures she has replaced Jesus in popular affections. The colourful feasts of Mary—in Europe we think of the Feast of her Assumption into Heaven on August 15th—brought joy into the lives of many, rich and poor alike, and still do.

On the other hand, she has been frequently used to control the lives of women. Specifically, the model of Virgin Mother has been used as a model. Pope John Paul II has proposed the spiritual motherhood of Mary as the ideal for being woman (John Paul II 1988). The liberation theologian Leonardo Boff (influenced by Jungian categories—and not for motives of control!), suggested an ontological link between women, Mary and the Holy Spirit (Boff 1989). This, he thought, would give

5.   See Grey (1989), Warner (1987), Cunneen (1996), Ruether (1977), Gebara and Bingemer (1989).

women a direct link to the Trinity! Mercifully, this has been shown to be theologically completely without justification (Coakley 1992). The storm that greeted Tissa Balasuriya's book, *Mary and Human Liberation* (1997) is sufficient evidence of the importance that the Vatican had placed in using Mariology to control the lives of women.

But the important point for this study is that now that there is such an interest in developing theologies of Mary from many perspectives, ecumenical, Jewish and Muslim, liberationist, and so on, this has freed her from being an instrument for control. It has not only freed her from having to be the female dimension of the divine—it has at the same time encouraged the exploration of this dimension for God. Most importantly she has been rediscovered in her biblical role as prophetic woman, as speaking up for the suffering of poor women (Gebara and Bingemer 1989).

Beyond God the Father—and Back Again?

This book began by expressing the urgency expressed in many contexts of moving beyond the traditional naming of God as male, as the patriarchal Father God. This was not only because of its lack of inclusivity, but because the 'name of the Father' guarantees the structuring of society, law and the cultural symbolic system in such a way as to keep women subordinate. There have been so many attempts to find a different way of naming God. Thus, Rosemary Ruether refers to the deity as God/ess. Elisabeth Schüssler Fiorenza's solution is to write of G*d. Neither of these solutions are helpful for prayer. Others simply address 'God', avoiding any personal pronoun. Attempts to replace 'He' with 'She' in public liturgies usually produce storms of protest. But there are now many creative attempts to address the deity in an inclusive way (Proctor-Smith 1995). Janet Morley's Collects written for Sundays throughout the year, for example (Morley 1988)—and invoking a richness of inclusive imagery—have even been used in English Cathedrals. But the point I make here is that the naming of God is deeply important to people. It is not surprising that it should be controversial because it touches the deepest chord of identity. Hence one of the clear directions for the future is to keep on praying and singing in this enriched, inclusive way and to discern the many connections between praying and living in a more just way.

Feminist liturgists need also to be open to the need to rediscover God the father. Not the patriarchal father, of course, but the caring and nurturing father—so widely needed in societies where fathers are absent, distant or abusive, and their sons lack good masculine role models. Feminist theologians in their anxiety to reclaim just patterns for motherhood need also to be generous in their understanding of the needs of young men as well as women. Far from a fall back into patriarchy, there is a reconstructing or reconfiguring of transformed patterns of maleness and femaleness: in the family context the focus is the creation of patterns of caring with shared authority and responsibility between men and women.[6]

God in Movement

The most crucial symbol for God in the Christian tradition is God as Trinity. I have been alluding to this several times, as well as developing a theology of the Spirit but have not discussed the Trinitarian God as such, partly because it would have needed a developed Christology, but mostly because of feminist methodology. This has never insisted on taking a traditional symbol and forcing it to be the centre of feminist thinking. And yet, in a strange way, without seeking for it, one could be astounded by the way the Trinity turns out to be at the heart of feminist theological thinking.

It is certainly not a Trinity of three men. Nor a Trinity of two men plus the Holy Spirit. (The two men and a pigeon caricature!) As I have indicated throughout, feminist theology refuses to carve up the deity in a gender-specific way. Even though goddess *thealogy* and ritual points to the Goddess in her three phases of Maiden–Mother–Wise Woman as honouring femaleness,[7] Christian theology does not adopt this iconography as replacing the old male Trinity. Trinitarian imagery arises in feminist theology in a variety of ways. First, it is ironic that Mary Daly, who is so scathing in her dismissal of the all-male Trinity (Daly 1973), seems still to adhere to a traditional threefold structure in her women-identified universe (Daly 1984). Thus, the movement is from 'archespheres', where women have to break out of patriarchal patterns, to 'pyrospheres', the spheres of passions and virtues, to 'metamorphosespheres', where—

---

6.   Although this is an urgent task, it falls outside the parameters of this book.
7.   See Raphael (1999) in this series.

according to Daly—women experience transformation, inspiration and
new empowering (1984: 411).

But more at the heart of Christian feminist thought, is that the per-
fection of Trinitarian love, and the dance of *perichoresis,* is reflected in
the theological privileging of relation, communion, mutuality, reciproc-
ity and connection.[8] Feminist Trinitarian thinking stresses a dynamic
God in movement (Grey 1990), but also sees suffering at the heart of
Trinity (Johnson 1994). If, as the late Catherine Lacugna argued, living
Trinitarian faith expresses both orthodoxy (praise of God) and ortho-
praxis (1991: 410), it is as lived ethical expression that I would characterize the strength of feminist Trinitarian thinking. Feminist ethical
thinking is always rooted in the urgency of the realities of women's
lives. So, when liturgical settings call on God as 'Creator, Redeemer,
Sustainer', it is a functional use of Trinitarian language to make direct
links with God's involvement with the struggles and sufferings of
women, their families and communities. As Jane Williams wrote:

> at the heart of Christian Trinitarian tradition is a vision of a *society*; a
> society that is based on mutuality, a society where personality is defined
> in relation rather than achievement, a society, in short, that is based on a
> vision of the society of the Trinity (Williams 1992: 41).[9]

The idea that *God is community* is also expressed by women's voices from
many contexts. Thus, Elizabeth Dominguez from the Philippines writes:

> To be in the image of God is to be in community. It is not simply a man
> or woman who can reflect God, but it is the community-in-relationship
> (Dominguez 1989: 87).

But it could also be said that God as Trinity expresses not only the
mutuality of relation between persons, but their distinctiveness, diversity, *otherness* and the need to respect this. That the other can be transformed from the *threatening* other, to the *beloved* other is a concern at the
heart of feminist theology. These words of Wendy Farley encapsulate
the link between the face of the other and the making of justice in
society:

---

8.   Yet it must also be noted that feminist theology explores other sorts of
plurality than the Trinitarian symbol.

9.   I am aware of the objections to this: 'the functional language of Creator,
Redeemer, Sustainer, is not exactly in accord with the biblical testimony that God
creates and redeems us through Jesus Christ by the power of the Holy Spirit'
(Lacugna 1993: 105).

> The plurality and ambiguity of our world, call us to a vigilant renuncia-
> tion of totality, of possession, of presence. But the face of the other, the
> beauty and vulnerability of nature, calls us to responsibility. Eros traverses
> the distance between renunciation and responsibility. If only we could
> forgo pornographies of truth and find the courage to subsist in this ten-
> sion, to embrace the securities and delights of a ceaseless desire for truth
> (W. Farley 1996: 200).

Believing in and praying to a Trinitarian God is keeping alive the hope
in a different kind of society, one where the fragile connections and
relations are treated with reverence, but where the tensions of difference
and otherness challenge the limits of law, structures and traditions.

To Let God be who God will be

There can be no doubt that the creative imagery springing from a
Christian feminist experience of God is a vibrant force. Even though
many of its expressions have been strictly outside the parameters of
official Church (and thousands of women have in any case left the
Church, bitter and alienated), the thousand women participants of the
European Women's Synod, Gmünden 1996—and many similar gather-
ings across the world—have strengthened or rediscovered faith in the
divine through the freedom and liberating imagination of the process.
Also, through the decade of Churches in Solidarity with Women (1988–
1998) and the commitment of the World Council of Churches since its
foundation (1948) to the situation of women globally, new expressions
of faith are entering 'mainstream' Church. This must be reckoned as a
sign of great hope for the institution.

But this process of new naming is far wider than the institution resisting categorization, as I have said. Feminist theology of God is both radical and traditional simultaneously. When Ntosoke Shange cries, 'I found
God within myself and I loved her, I loved her fiercely' (Shange 1976),
she is close to Augustine's cry, '*Deus intimior intima meo*'.[10] The difference is that a black woman has uttered her own discovery and her cry is
affirming her own bodiliness in a culture which has often despised it.

Again, the revelation of the beauty of God, and sheer delight in the
myriad relations of this in creation is also rooted in the mystical tradition
of the Church. So when Edwina Gateley speaks of a 'warm, moist, salty
God', 'stirring in my guts, quickening my middle-aged bones' (Gateley

---

10. 'God is closer to me than my deepest self'.

1993: 90), there are also many parallels, ancient and contemporary. If there is a linking point in feminist thought about God it is what I call the *enacting, transforming dimension*. Christian feminist theologians, in the way they call on God, not only express the connections between images and symbols and the world we inhabit, but want to change and transform it by their naming. They know that this transformation is not achieved by the mere replacing of 'he' by 'she'. The new naming calls for a radically new symbolization and meaning-making process, transcending the old dualisms, whereby 'woman', 'nature', 'body' and 'immanence' are the shadow and inferior side of the split. This process is open-ended but has already begun. There is a growing confidence that it is possible to live now and to be transformed now—personally and communally—within the vision of the *kin-dom*[11] of this relational God, enacting our vision because we are empowered by the countless revelations of the presence of the divine: this vulnerable, tragic God, immanent in embodied life-on-earth, sustaining and energizing our passion for justice; yet ever transcendent, as She weaves in and out of our communities, crossing and re-crossing boundaries, opening our hearts to each other and to all life forms, pouring out compassionate love and an unquenchable hope that *all will be well, all will be well* for the most forsaken and rejected of the world. For, in the end, God will be God, and the world will find its true homecoming into God. Hospitality, hearth-welcome, heart-room, find their roots and fulfilment in this divine reality, source of our deepest yearnings and our wildest dreams. Yes, we are told, *the journey is home,* but home is here and God is here, incarnate in all the chaos of our communal life. But, we take heart, for

> Even in the chaos you will bear me up;
> if the waters go over my head,
> you will be holding me.
> For the chaos is yours also,
> and in the swirling of the mighty waters
> is your presence known (Morley 1988: 50).

---

11. '*kin-dom*'—a word issuing from Mujerista theology means that we are all *kith and kin*, brothers and sisters in the new creation.

Bibliography

Aquino, Maria Pilar
    1993   *Our Cry for Life: Feminist Theology from Latin America* (Maryknoll, NY: Orbis Books).
    1998   'Latin American Feminist Theology', *Journal of Feminist Studies of Religion* 14: 1, 89–107.

Arellano, Beatriz
    1988   'Women's Experience of God in Emerging Spirituality', in Fabella and Oduyoye 1988: 135-50.

Avis, Paul
    1989   *Eros and the Sacred* (London: SPCK).

Baker, Ella, and Marvel Cooke
    1935   'The Bronx Slave Market', *The Crisis* 42: 330-331, also cited in Grant 1993: 206.

Balasuriya, Tissa
    1997   *Mary and Human Liberation* (London: Cassell).

Baltazar, Stella
    1996   'Domestic Violence in Indian Perspective', in Mananzan and Oduyoye *et al.* 1996: 56-65.

Beauvoir, Simone de
    1973   *The Second Sex* (Harmondsworth: Penguin Books).

Becker, Ernst
    1973   *The Denial of Death* (trans. Sir Tobie Matthew; New York: Free Press).

Beckman, Ninna
    1997   'Sophia, Symbol of Christian and Feminist Wisdom?', *Feminist Theology* 16: 32-54.

Berry, Thomas
    1999   *The Great Work* (New York: Bell Tower).

Binford, Sally
    1982   'Are Goddesses and Matriarchies Merely Figments of Feminist Imagination?', in Spretnak 1982: 541-49.

Bingemer, Maria Clara
    1989   'Reflections on the Trinity', in Tamez 1989: 56-80.

Bitton-Jackson, Livia
    1982   *Madonna or Courtesan? The Jewish Woman in Christian Literature* (New York: Seabury Press).

Boff, Leonardo
    1989   *The Maternal Face of God* (London: Collins).

Boyce-Tillman, June
    1996   *European Women Synod, Lieder-Songs* (Austria: Gmunden).

Brock, Rita Nakashima
    1988   *Journeys by Heart: A Christology of Erotic Power* (New York: Crossroads).
Buber, Martin
    1939   *I and Thou* (ed. and trans. W. Kaufmann; Edinburgh: T. & T. Clark).
Camp, Claudia
    1995   'Wise and Strange: An Interpretation of the Female Imagery in Proverbs in Light of Trickster Mythology', in Athalya Brenner (ed.), *A Feminist Companion to Wisdom Literature* (Sheffield: Sheffield Academic Press): 131-56.
Cannon, Katie Geneva
    1985   'Kate and the Color Purple', in The Mudflower Collective 1985: 104-105.
    1988   *Black Womanist Ethics* (Atlanta: Scholars Press).
    1989   'Moral Wisdom in the Black Women's Tradition', in Plaskow and Christ 1989: 281-92.
Carr, Anne
    1988   *Transforming Grace: Christian Tradition and Women's Experience* (New York: Harper SanFrancisco).
Christ, Carol
    1979   'Why Women Need the Goddess: Phenomenological, Psychological and Political Reflections', in Christ and Plaskow 1979: 273-88.
    1980   *Diving Deep and Surfacing: Women Writers on Spiritual Quest* (Boston: Beacon Press).
    1987   *The Laughter of Aphrodite: Reflections in a Journey to the Goddess* (San Francisco: Harper & Row).
    1995   *Odyssey with the Goddess: A Spiritual Quest in Crete* (New York: Continuum).
    1997   *Rebirth of the Goddess: Finding Meaning in Feminist Spirituality* (New York: Addison-Wesley Publishing).
Christ, Carol, and Judith Plaskow (eds.)
    1979   *Womanspirit Rising: A Feminist Reader in Religion* (New York: Harper & Row): 273-88.
Christian, Barbara
    1980   *Black Women Novelists: The Development of a Tradition (1892-1976)* (Westport, CT: Greenwood Press).
Chung, Hyun Kyung
    1993   *Struggle to be the Sun Again* (Maryknoll, NY: Orbis Books).
    1996   'Your Comfort vs. My Death', in Mananzan *et al.* 1996: 129-40.
Clinebell, Howard
    1996   *Ecotherapy: Healing Ourselves, Healing the Earth* (Augsburg: Fortress Press).
Coakley, Sarah
    1988   'Femininity and the Holy Spirit', in Furlong 1988: 124-35.
    1992   'Mariology and "Romantic Feminism": A Critique', in Elwes 1992: 97-110.
    1996   'Kenosis and Subversion', in Hampson 1996: 82-111.
Cobb, John
    1981   'Feminism and Process Thought: A Two-Way Relationship', in Davaney 1981: 32-61.

Cobb, John, and David Griffin
  1976   *Process Theology: An Introductory Exposition* (Philadelphia: Westminster Press).
Cohn-Sherbok, Dan
  1989   *Holocaust Theology* (London: Marshall, Morgan & Scott).
Cole, Susan, Marian Ronan and Hal Taussig (eds.)
  1996   *Wisdom's Feast: Sophia in Study and Celebration* (Kansas City: Sheed and Ward, 2nd edn).
Colledge E. OSA, and J. Walsh SJ (eds.)
  1978   *Julian of Norwich: Showings, Classics of Western Spirituality* (London: SPCK; New York: Paulist).
Cotter, Jim
  1983   *Prayer at Night: A Book for the Darkness* (Exeter and London: Cotter J. amd Pelz P.).
  1999   *Dazzling Darkness* (Sheffield: Cairns Publications).
Cox, Harvey
  1974   *The Seduction of the Spirit* (New York: Random House).
  1997   *Fire from Heaven* (London: Cassell).
Craighead, Meinrad
  1986   *The Mother's Songs* (Mahwah, NJ: Paulist Press).
Cronon, William (ed.)
  1995   *Uncommon Ground: Toward Reinventing Nature* (New York: W. & W. Norton).
Cunneen, Sally
  1996   *In Search of Mary: The Woman and the Symbol* (New York: Ballantine Books).
Daly, Mary
  1973   *Beyond God the Father* (London: The Women's Press).
  1984   *Pure Lust* (London: The Women's Press).
Daly, M., and J. Caputi (eds.)
  1988   *Wickedary* (London: The Women's Press).
Davaney, Sheila Greave (ed.)
  1981   *Feminism and Process Thought* (Lewiston, NY: Edwin Mellen Press).
Deane-Drummond, Celia
  1997   'Sophia: the Feminine Face of God as a Metaphor for an Ecotheology', *Feminist Theology* 16: 11-31.
  1998   *Theology and Biotechnology* (London and Washington: Geoffrey Chapman).
Derks, M., J. Eijt, and M. Monteiro (eds.)
  1997   *Sterven voor de wereld: Een religieus ideaal in meervoud*, I (Metamorfosen. Studies in religieuze geschiedenis; Hilversum; Verloren).
Diamond, Irene, and Gloria Feman Orenstein (eds.)
  1990   *Reweaving the World: The Emergence of Ecofeminism* (San Francisco: Sierra Club Books).
Dietrich, Gabriel
  1998   'The World as the Body of God: Feminist Perspectives on Ecology and Social Justice', in *Ecotheology* 5 and 6 (Sheffield: Sheffield Academic Press): 25-50.
Dominguez, Elizabeth
  1989   'Biblical Concept of Human Sexuality: Challenge to Tourism', in Fabella and Sun Ai 1989: 83-91.

Downing, Christine
    1989   'Artemis', in Plaskow and Christ 1989: 119-27.

Eller, Cynthia
    1996   'Wicca/Neopaganism', in Letty M. Russell and J. Shannon Clarkson (eds.), *Dictionary of Feminist Theologies* (London: Mowbray): 314.

Elwes, Teresa (ed.)
    1992   *Women's Voices: Essays in Contemporary Feminist Theology* (London: Marshall Pickering).

European Women's Synod
    1996   *Lieder-Songs-Chansons* (Austria: Gmünden).

Fabella, Virginia, and Mercy Amba Oduyoye (eds.)
    1988   *With Passion and Compassion: Third World Women doing Theology* (Maryknoll, NY: Orbis Books).

Fabella, Virginia, and Sergio Torres (eds.)
    1985   *Doing Theology in a Divided World* (Maryknoll, NY: Orbis Books).

Fabella, Virginia, and Sun-Ai Lee Park (eds.)
    1989   *We Dare to Dream: Doing Theology as Asian Women* (Hong Kong: Asian Women's Resource Centre for Culture and Theology).

Falk, Marcia
    1989   'Towards a Jewish Feminist Reconstruction of Monotheism', *Tikkun* 4, Part 4: 53-56.
    1989a   'Notes on Composing New Blessings', in Plaskow and Christ 1989: 128-38.

Farley, Edward
    1996   *Divine Empathy: A Theology of God and Compassion: Good and Evil* (Augsberg: Fortress Press).

Farley, Wendy
    1990   *Tragic Vision and Divine Compassion: A Contemporary Theodicy* (Louisville, KY: Westminster/John Knox Press).
    1996   *Eros for the Other: Retaining Truth in a Pluralistic World* (University Park, PA: Pennsylvania State University Press).

Fox, Matthew
    1981   *Whee! We, Wee All the Way Home: A Guide to a Sensual, Prophetic Spirituality* (Santa Fe: Bear and Co.).
    1983   *Original Blessing: A Primer in Creation Spirituality* (Santa Fe: Bear and Co.).

Furlong, Monica (ed.)
    1988   *Mirror to the Church* (London: SPCK).

Gadon, Elinor
    1989   *The Once and Future Goddess* (San Francisco: Harper & Row).

Galloway, Cathy
    1993   *Love Burning Deep* (London: SPCK).

Gateley, Edwina
    1993   *A Warm, Moist, Salty God: Women Journeying Toward Wisdom* (Trabaco Canyon: Source Books).

Gebara, Yvone
    1989   'Women Doing Theology in Latin America', in Tamez 1989: 37-48.

Gebara, Yvone, and Bingemer, Maria Clara
    1989   *Mary, Mother of God, Mother of the Poor* (Maryknoll, NY: Orbis Books).

Gimbutas, Maria
   1989   *The Language of the Goddess* (San Francisco: Harper & Row).
   1989a   'Women and Culture in Goddess-oriented old Europe', in Plaskow and
               Christ 1989: 63-71.
Gnanadason, Aruna
   1988   'Women's Oppression—A Sinful Situation', in Fabella and Oduyoye
               1988: 67-76.
Gottlieb, Lynn
   1982   'Speaking into the Silence', *Response* 41-42: 23, 27.
Grant, Jacqueline
   1989   *White Women's Christ and Black Women's Jesus* (Atlanta: Scholars Press).
   1993   'The Sin of Servanthood and the Deliverance of Discipleship', in Townes
               1993: 199-218.
Grey, Mary
   1989   *Redeeming the Dream: Christianity, Feminism and Redemption* (London:
               SPCK).
   1989a   'Reclaiming Mary: A Task for Feminist Theology', *The Way*, 29.4: 334-
               40.
   1990   'The Core of Our Desire: Reclaiming the Trinity', *Theology*, September/
               October: 363-72.
   1993   *The Wisdom of Fools? Seeking Revelation Today* (London: SPCK).
   1993a   'From Cultures of Silence to Cosmic Justice-making: A Way Forward for
               Theology?' (Southampton: University of Southampton).
   1997   *Beyond the Dark Night: A Way Forward for the Church* (London: Cassell).
   1997a   *Prophecy and Mysticism: The Heart of the Postmodern Church* (Edinburgh: T.
               & T. Clark).
   1997b   'Who do you say that I am? Images of Christ in Feminist Liberation
               Theology', in Stanley E. Porter, Michael A. Hayes and David Tombs
               (eds.), *Images of Christ: Ancient and Modern* (Sheffield: Sheffield Academic
               Press): 189-203.
   1997c   'Empowered to Lead: Sophia's Daughters Blaze a Trail', in Martin,
               McEwan and Tatman 1997: 91-106.
   1998   'The Decline and Fall of the Second Millennium: Final Chapter or New
               Beginning for Christianity?', *New Blackfriars* 79.931 (September): 337-64.
   2000   *The Outrageous Pursuit of Hope: Prophetic Dreams for the 21st Century*
               (London: Darton, Longman & Todd).
Grey, Mary (ed.)
   1995   *Theology in Green*, II (Southampton: La Sainte Union).
Grey, M., A. Heaton and D.A. Sullivan (eds.)
   1994   *The Candles are still Burning* (London: Cassell).
Grey, M., and R. Zipfel
   1993   *From Barriers to Community* (London: HarperCollins, 1993).
Griffin, Susan
   1978   *Woman and Nature: The Roaring Inside Her* (New York: Harper & Row).
   1989   'The Earth is my Sister', in Plaskow and Christ 1989: 105-110.
Grigg, Richard
   1994   'Enacting the Divine: Feminist Theology and the being of God', in *Journal
               of Religion* 74.4: 506-23.

Gross, Rita
    1978   'Hindu Female Deities as a Resource for Discovering the Goddess', *Journal of the American Academy of Religion* 46.3: 269-91.
    1979   'Female God Language in a Jewish Context', in Christ and Plaskow 1979: 167-73.
Halkes, Catherina
    1997   'Sterven om te leven', in Derks, Eijt and Monteiro 1997: 125-36.
Hampson, Daphne (ed.)
    1996   *Swallowing the Fishbone* (London: SPCK).
Hartshorne, Charles
    1948   *The Divine Reality: A Social Concept of God* (New Haven: Yale University Press).
Haskins, Susan
    1993   *Mary Magdalen* (New York: HarperCollins).
Hebblethwaite, Margaret
    1984   *Motherhood and God* (London: Geoffrey Chapman).
Heyward, Carter
    1982   *The Redemption of God: A Theology of Mutuality* (Washington, DC: University of America Press).
    1984   *Our Passion for Justice* (New York: Pilgrim).
    1989   *Touching our Strength: The Erotic as Power and Love of God* (San Francisco: Harper & Row).
Hick, John
    1985   *Evil and the God of Love* (London: MacMillan [1968]).
Hillesum, Etty
    1985   *An Interrupted Life: The Diaries of Etty Hillesum 1941–43* (New York: Washington Square Press).
Hopkins, Gerard Manley
    1953   *Poems and Prose* (Harmondsworth: Penguin Books), selected by W.H. Gardner.
Hughes, Gerard
    1996   *God of Surprises* (London: Darton, Longman & Todd [1985]).
Hunter, Patricia
    1993   'Women's Power, Women's Passion', in Townes 1993: 189-98.
Hurcombe, Linda (ed.)
    1987   *Sex and God: Some Varieties of Women's Religious Experience* (New York and London: Routledge and Kegan Paul).
Hurston, Zora Neale
    1990   *Their Eyes were Watching God* (New York: Harper & Row [1937]).
Irigaray, Luce
    1987   'Femmes Divines', in *Sexes et Parentés* (repr.; Paris: Editions de Minuit): 69-85.
Isasi-Diaz, Ada Maria
    1993   *En La Lucha/In the Struggle: Elaborating a Mujerista Theology* (Minneapolis: Fortress Press).
Isherwood, Lisa, and Elizabeth Stuart
    1998   *Introducing Body Theology* (Sheffield: Sheffield Academic Press).

Isherwood, Lisa, and Dorothea McEwan (eds.)
    1996   *An A to Z of Feminist Theology* (Sheffield: Sheffield Academic Press).
Jantzen, Grace
    1984   *God's World, God's Body* (London: Darton, Longman & Todd [1981]).
    1987   *Julian of Norwich* (London: SPCK).
    1998   *Becoming Divine: Towards a Feminist Philosophy of Religion* (Manchester: Manchester University Press).
Jeanrond, Werner, and Jennifer Rike (eds.)
    1991   *Radical Pluralism and Truth* (New York: Crossroads).
John Paul II
    1988   *Mulieris Dignitatem* (London: The Catholic Truth Society).
Johnson, Elizabeth
    1994   *She Who Is: The Mystery of God in Feminist Theological Discourse* (New York: Crossroads).
Julian of Norwich
    1966   *Revelations of Divine Love* (Harmondsworth: Penguin Books).
Keen, Sam
    1983   *The Passionate Life: Stages of Loving* (San Francisco: Harper & Row).
Kellenbach, Katharina von
    1994   *Anti-Judaism in Feminist Religious Writing* (Atlanta: Scholars Press).
Keller, Catherine
    1986   *From a Broken Web: Separation, Sexism and Self* (Boston: Beacon Press).
    1990   'Women against Wasting the World: Notes on Eschatology and Ecology', in Diamond and Orenstein 1990: 249-63.
    1995   'Power Lines', *Theology Today* 5.2: 188-203.
    1996   *Apocalypse Now and Then: A Feminist Story of the End of the World* (Boston: Beacon Press).
King, Ursula
    1989   *Women and Spirituality: Voices of Protest and Promise* (London: MacMillan Education).
King, Ursula (ed.)
    1994   *Feminist Theology from the Third World: A Reader* (London: SPCK).
Kloppenberg, John S.
    1982   'Isis and Sophia in the Book of Wisdom', *Harvard Theological Review* 75: 57-84.
Kristeva, Julia
    1982   *Powers of Horror: An Essay on Abjection* (trans. Leon S. Roudiez; New York: Columbia University Press).
Kwok, Pui Lan
    1986   'God weeps with our Pain', in Pobee and von Wärtenburg-Potter 1986: 90-95.
Lacugna, Catherine Mowry
    1991   *God for Us: The Trinity and Christian Life* (New York: HarperCollins).
Lacugna, Catherine Mowry (ed.)
    1993   *Freeing Theology: The Essentials of Theology in Feminist Perspective* (New York: HarperCollins).
Lash, Nicholas
    1991   'Conversation in Gethsemane', in Jeanrond and Rike 1991: 51-61.

Long, Asphodel
    1992   *In a Chariot Drawn by Lions: The Search for the Female in Deity* (London: The Women's Press).

Mananzan, M.J., and Tamez Oduyoye *et al.* (eds.)
    1996   *Women Resisting Violence: Spirituality for Life* (Maryknoll, NY: Orbis Books).

Martin, F., D. McEwan and L. Tatman
    1997   *Cymbals and Silences: Echoes from the First European Women's Synod* (London: Sophia Press).

Matthews, Caitlin
    1991   *Sophia, Goddess of Wisdom: The Divine Feminine from Black Goddess to World Soul* (London: Grafton/Mandala).

McFague, Sally
    1982   *Metaphorical Theology: Models of God in Religious Language* (London: SCM Press).
    1987   *Models of God: Theology for an Ecological Nuclear Age* (London: SCM Press).
    1993   *The Body of God: An Ecological Theology* (London: SCM Press).
    1997   *Super, Natural Christians: How we should Love Nature* (London: SCM Press).

McIntyre, Alasdair
    1981   *After Virtue* (London: Gerald Duckworth).

Merchant, Carolyn
    1980   *The Death of Nature: Women, Ecology and the Scientific Revolution* (San Francisco: Harper & Row).
    1995   'Reinventing Eden: Western Culture as a Recovery Narrative', in Cronon 1995: 133-59.

Mollenkott, Virginia
    1983   *The Divine Feminine* (New York: Crossroads).

Moltmann, Jürgen
    1974   *The Crucified God* (trans. John Bowden; London: SCM Press).
    1981   'The Motherly Father: Is Trinitarian Patripassianism replacing Theological Patriarchalism?', in Schillebeeckx and Metz 1981: 51-56.

Moody, Linda
    1996   *Women Encounter God: Theology across the Boundaries of Difference* (Maryknoll, NY: Orbis Books).

Morley, Janet
    1988   *All Desires Known* (London: Movement for the Ordination of Women; Women in Theology).

Morrison, Toni
    1970   *The Bluest Eye* (New York: Washington Square Press).
    1987   *Beloved* (London: Chatto and Windus).

Morton, Nelle
    1985   *The Journey is Home* (Boston: Beacon Press).
    1989   'The Goddess as Metaphoric Image', in Plaskow and Christ 1989: 11-118.

The Mudflower Collective
    1985   *God's Fierce Whimsy* (New York: Pilgrim).

Murdoch, Iris
    1970   *The Sovereignty of the Good* (London: Ark Paperbacks).

Musurillo, H.
    1972   *The Acts of the Christian Martyrs* (Oxford: Clarendon Press).

Newman, Barbara
    1995   *From Virile Woman to WomanChrist: Studies in Mediaeval Religion and
             Literature* (Philadelphia: University of Pennslyvania).
Nussbaum, Martha
    1986   *The Fragility of Goodness* (Cambridge: Cambridge University Press).
Oduyoye, Mercy Amba
    2001   *Introducing African Women's Theology* (Sheffield: Sheffield Academic Press).
Otto, Rudolf
    1958   *The Idea of the Holy* (trans. John Harvey; London: SPCK [1923]).
Owen, H.P.
    1971   *Concepts of Deity* (London: Macmillan).
Page, Ruth
    1985   *Ambiguity and the Presence of God* (London: SCM Press).
Patai, Raphael
    1967   *The Hebrew Goddess* (New York: Ktav).
Plaskow, Judith
    1982   'God and Feminism', *Menorah* 3 (February): 2.
    1989   'Jewish Memory from a Feminist Perspective', in Plaskow and Christ
             1989: 39-50.
    1990   *Standing Again at Sinai: Judaism from a Feminist Perspective* (San Francisco:
             Harper & Row).
    1991   'Feminist Anti-Judaism and the Christian God', *Journal of Feminist Studies
             in Religion* 7.2: 99-108.
Plaskow, Judith, and Carol Christ (eds.)
    1989   *Weaving the Visions: New Patterns in Feminist Spirituality* (San Francisco:
             Harper & Row).
Pobee, John S., and Bärbel von Wärtenburg-Potter
    1986   *New Eyes for Reading: Biblical and Theological Reflections by Women from the
             Third World* (Geneva: World Council of Churches).
Porter, Stanley E. (ed.)
    1997   *Images of Christ* (Sheffield: Sheffield Academic Press).
Porter, Stanley, and Philip Richter (eds.)
    1995   *Toronto Blessing—or is it?* (London: Darton, Longman & Todd).
Potok, Chaim
    1972   *My Name is Asher Lev* (New York: Heinemann).
Prado, Consuelo del
    1989   'I sense God in another Way', in Tamez 1989: 140-49.
Pratt, Ianthe
    1997   *Inclusive Language: Faith Community-God-Talk-Creative Worship* (London:
             Association for Inclusive Language; Christian Women's Resource Centre).
Proctor-Smith, Marjorie
    1995   *Praying with our Eyes Open: Engendering Feminist Liturgical Prayer* (Nashville:
             Abingdon Press).
Raphael, Melissa
    1999   *Introducing Thealogy* (Sheffield: Sheffield Academic Press).
Rich, Adrienne
    1976   *Of Woman Born* (New York: Bantam).
    1978   *The Dream of a Common Language: Poems* (New York: W. & W. Norton).

1980   'Integrity', in *idem*, *A Wild Patience has Taken me thus far: Poems 1978-1981*
            (New York: W. & W. Norton): 8-9.
Rosaldo, M.Z., and L. Lamphere (eds.)
1974   *Women, Culture and Society* (Stanford: Stanford University Press).
Ruether, Rosemary Radford
1977   *Mary, the Feminine Face of the Church* (Philadelphia: Westminster Press).
1983   *Sexism and God-Talk* (London: SCM Press).
1985   *Women-Church: Theology and Practice of Feminist Liturgical Communities* (San
            Francisco: Harper & Row).
1992   *Gaia and God: An Ecofeminist Theology of Earth Healing* (San Francisco:
            HarperCollins).
Ruprecht, Louis
1994   *Tragic Posture and Tragic Vision: Against the Modern Failure of Nerve* (New
            York: Continuum).
Russell, Letty
1993   *Church in the Round* (Louisville, KY: Westminster/John Knox Press).
Sands, Kathleen
1994   *Escape from Paradise* (Minneapolis: Fortress Press).
Schillebeeckx E., and J. Metz (eds.)
1981   *Concilium* (Edinburgh: T. & T. Clark).
Schroer, Silvia
1991   'Die göttliche Weisheit und der nachexilische Monotheismus', in Wacker
            and Zenger 1991: 151-83.
1995   'The Book of Sophia', in E. Schüssler Fiorenza (ed.), *Searching the Scrip-
            tures: A Feminist Commentary* (London: SCM Press): 17-38.
Schüssler, Elisabeth Fiorenza
1995   *Jesus, Miriam's Child, Sophia's Prophet* (London: SCM Press).
Scott, Joan
1997   'Women's Narratives of Slavery as Sacred Text' (Lecture at European
            Society of Women in Theological Research [ESWTR], Orthodox
            Academy, Crete).
Sen, Mala
1991   *India's Bandit Queen: The True Story of Phoolan Devi* (New Delhi: Harper-
            Collins India).
Shange, Ntosake
1976   *For coloured girls who have considered suicide/when the rainbow is enuf* (New
            York: Collier).
Soelle, Dorothee
1995   *Theology for Sceptics* (trans. Joyce I. Irwin; London: Mowbray).
Soskice, Janet Martin
1985   *Metaphor and Religious Language* (Oxford: Clarendon Press).
1992   'Can a Feminist Call God "Father"?', in Elwes 1992: 15-30.
Soskice, Janet Martin (ed.)
1990   *After Eve: Women, Theology and the Christian Tradition* (London: Marshall
            Pickering).
Spretnak, Charlene (ed.)
1982   *The Politics of Women's Spirituality* (New York: Doubleday).

Starhawk
  1989   *The Spiral Dance: The Rebirth of the Ancient Religion of the Goddesses* (San Francisco: Harper & Row).
Steen, Marc
  1989   'The Theme of the Suffering God', in J. Lambrecht and R. Collins (eds.), *God and Human Suffering* (Leuven: Peeters): 69-93.
Stuart, Elizabeth
  1992   *Daring to Speak Love's Name: A Gay and Lesbian Prayer Book* (London: Hamish Hamilton).
  1995   *Just Good Friends: Towards Lesbian and Gay Theology of Relationships* (London: Mowbray).
Styron, William
  1979   *Sophie's Choice* (New York: Random House).
Suchocki, Marjorie
  1988   *God, Christ and Church* (New York: Crossroads).
Tamez, Elsa
  1982   *The Bible of the Oppressed* (trans. Mathew O'Connell; Maryknoll, NY: Orbis Books).
  1985   'Letter to Job', in Fabella and Torres 1985: 175.
  1986   'The Woman who Complicated the History of Salvation', in Pobee and Wärtenberg-Potter 1986: 5-17.
Tamez, Elsa (ed.)
  1989   *Through her Eyes: Women's Theology from Latin America* (Maryknoll, NY: Orbis Books).
Tatman, Lucy
  1996   'Wisdom', in Isherwood and McEwan 1996: 236-38.
Taylor, John
  1972   *The Go-Between God* (London: Collins).
Taylor, Mark Kline
  1993   *Remembering Esperanza: A Cultural and Political Theology for North American Praxis* (Maryknoll, NY: Orbis Book).
Tepedino, Ana Maria
  1988   'Feminist Theology as the Fruit of Passion and Compassion', in Fabella and Oduyoye 1988: 165-72.
Thistlethwaite, Susan
  1990   *Sex, Race and God: Christian Feminism in Black and White* (London: Geoffrey Chapman).
  1996   'Militarism in N. American Perspective', in Mananzan and Oduyoye et al. 1996: 119-25.
Townes, Emilie M.
  1989   'Christian Ethics and Theology in Womanist Perspective', *Journal of Feminist Studies in Religion* 5.2: 94-97.
Townes, Emilie (ed.)
  1993   *A Troubling in my Soul: Womanist Perspectives on Evil and Suffering* (Maryknoll, NY: Orbis Books).
Trible, Phyllis
  1978   *God and the Rhetoric of Sexuality* (Philadelphia: Fortress Press).

Umansky, Ellen M.
  1989   'Creating a Jewish Feminist Theology', in Plaskow and Christ 1989: 187-
            98.
Wacker, Marie-Theres, and Erich Zenger (eds.)
  1991   *Der Eine Gott unter Die Göttin: Gottesvorstellungen des biblisches Israel im
            Horizont feministischer Theologie* (Questiones Disputatae, 135; Freiburg:
            Herder).
Walker, Alice
  1982   *Meridian* (London: The Women's Press).
  1983   *The Color Purple* (London: The Women's Press).
  1983a   *In Search of our Mothers' Gardens* (London: The Women's Press).
Walker Bynum, Caroline
  1982   *Jesus as Mother: Studies in the Spirituality of the High Middle Ages* (Berkeley:
            University of California Press).
  1997   *Holy Feast and Holy Fast: The Religious Significance of Food to Mediaeval
            Women* (Berkeley: University of California Press).
Warner, Marina
  1987   *Alone of all her Sex: The Myth and the Cult of the Virgin Mary* (London:
            Picador).
Wehr, Demaris
  1988   *Jung and Feminism: Liberating Archetypes* (London: Routledge).
Weil, Simone
  1950   *Waiting on God* (trans. Emma Crawford; London: Collins; Fontana).
Welch, Sharon
  1990   *A Feminist Ethic of Risk* (Minneapolis: Augsburg–Fortress).
Whitehead, Alfred North
  1924   *Process and Reality* (Cambridge: Macmillan).
Whitmont, Edward
  1980   *The Return of the Goddess* (New York: Bantam).
Wiesel, Eli
  1977   *The Trial of God* (New York: Random House).
Williams, Dolores
  1989   'Womanist Theology: Black Women's Voices', in Plaskow and Christ
            1989: 179-86.
  1993   *Sisters in the Wilderness: The Challenge of Womanist God-Talk* (Maryknoll,
            NY: Orbis Books).
Williams, Jane
  1992   'The Doctrine of the Trinity—A Way Forward for Feminists?', in Elwes
            1992: 31-43.
Wilson-Kastner, P., G.R. Kastner *et al.* (eds.)
  1981   'The Martyrdom of Perpetua: A Protest Account of Early Christianity', in
            P. Wilson-Kastner and G.R. Kastner (eds.), *A Lost Tradition: Women Writers
            of the Early Church* (Washington, DC: University Press of America): 1-32.
Wootton, Janet
  2000   *Introducing Christian Feminist Liturgy* (Sheffield: Sheffield Academic Press).
Wren, Brian
  1989   *What Images Shall I Borrow? God-Talk in Worship: A Male Response to
            Feminist Theology* (London: SCM Press).

INDEXES

INDEX OF REFERENCES

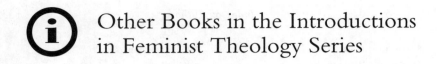 Other Books in the Introductions
in Feminist Theology Series

INTRODUCING ASIAN FEMINIST THEOLOGY
KWOK PUI-LAN

The book introduces the history, critical issues, and direction of feminist theology as a grass roots movement in Asia. Kwok Pui-Lan takes care to highlight the diversity of this broad movement, noting that not all women theologians in Asia embrace feminism. Amid a diverse range of sociopolitical, religiocultural, postcultural, and postcolonial context, this book lifts up the diversity of voices and ways of doing feminist theology while attending to women's experiences, how the Bible is interpreted, and the ways that Asian religious traditions are appropriated. It searches out a passionate, life-affirming spirituality through feminine images of God, new metaphors for Christ, and reformulation of sin and redemption.
ISBN 0 8298 1399-3   Paper/136 pages/$16.95

INTRODUCING THEALOGY: DISCOURSE ON THE
GODDESS
MELISSA RAPHAEL

Introducing Thealogy provides an accessible but critical introduction to the relationship of religion, theo/alogy, and gender especially as these concepts unfold in the revival of Goddess religion among feminists in Europe, North America, and Australasia. Raphael focuses on the boundaries of that broad movement, what is meant by the Goddess, theology in history and ethics, the political implications of the movement, and how it relates to feminist witchcraft.
ISBN 0 8298 1379-9   Paper/184 pages/$17.95

INTRODUCING BODY THEOLOGY
LISA ISHERWOOD AND ELIZABETH STUART

Because Christianity asserts that God was incarnated in human form, one might expect that its theologies would be body affirming. Yet for women (and indeed also for gay men) the body has been the site for oppression. *Introducing Body Theology* offers a body-centered theology that discusses cosmology, ecology, ethics, immortality, and sexuality, in a concise introduction that proposes and encourages a positive theology of the body.

ISBN 0 8298 1375-6   Paper/168 pages/$16.95

INTRODUCING A PRACTICAL FEMINIST THEOLOGY OF WORSHIP
JANET WOOTTON

Only three great women-songs are retained in the Bible: Deborah's song for ordinary people, Hannah's song of triumph, and Mary's song at meeting her cousin Elizabeth.

Many others, such as Miriam's song, are truncated or overshadowed by male triumphs. *Introducing a Practical Feminist Theology of Worship* begins by revealing how women have been 'whispering liturgy'. It then explores female images of God, discusses how worship spaces function, and offers practical suggestions for how women can use words and movements to construct authentic forms of worship.

ISBN 0 8298 1405-1   Paper/148 pages/$16.95

INTRODUCING REDEMPTION IN CHRISTIAN FEMINISM
ROSEMARY R. RUETHER

Introducing Redemption in Christian Feminism explores the dichotomy between two patterns of thinking found in Christianity: the redemption of Christ being applied to all without regard to gender, and the exclusion of women from leadership because women were created subordinate to men and because women were more culpable for sin. After examining these two patterns, Ruether examines some key theological themes: Christology, the self, the cross, and eschatology.

ISBN 0 8298 1382-9   Paper/136 pages/$15.95

INTRODUCING AFRICAN WOMEN'S THEOLOGY
MERCY AMBA ODUYOYE

Mercy Amba Oduyoye describes the context and methodology of Christian theology by Africans in the past two decades, offering brief descriptions of sample treatments of theological issues such as creation, Christology, ecclesiology, and eschatology.

The daily spiritual life of African Christina women is evident as the reader is led to the sources of African women's Christian theology. This book reflects how African culture and its multi-religious context has influenced women's selection of theological issues.
ISBN 0 8298 1423-X   Paper/156 pages/$17.00

INTRODUCING FEMINIST IMAGES OF GOD
MARY GREY

Mary Grey presents recent thinking reflecting early attempts to move beyond restrictive God language, opening up the possibilities of more inclusive ways of praying. The rich experiences of God, distinctive and diverse, are seen through the eyes of many different cultures and the women who struggle for justice. Using the figure of Sophia Wisdom as an example, Grey shows that there are many still unplumbed images of God to discover.
ISBN 0 8298 1418-3   Paper/148 pages/$17.00

To order call 1-800-537-3394, fax 216-736-2206,
or visit our Web site at www.pilgrimpress.com.
(Prices do not include shipping and handling.) Prices subject to change
without notice.